How to Read Journal Articles in the Social Sciences

SAGE Study Skills

How to Read Journal Articles in the Social Sciences

A Very Practical Guide for Students

2nd Edition

Phillip Chong Ho Shon

Los Angeles | London | New Delhi
Singapore | Washington DC | Boston

Los Angeles | London | New Delhi
Singapore | Washington DC | Boston

SAGE Publications Ltd
1 Oliver's Yard
55 City Road
London EC1Y 1SP

SAGE Publications Inc.
2455 Teller Road
Thousand Oaks, California 91320

SAGE Publications India Pvt Ltd
B 1/I 1 Mohan Cooperative Industrial Area
Mathura Road
New Delhi 110 044

SAGE Publications Asia-Pacific Pte Ltd
3 Church Street
#10-04 Samsung Hub
Singapore 049483

Editor: Jai Seaman
Assistant editor: Lily Mehrbod
Production editor: Tom Bedford
Copyeditor: Andy Baxter
Proofreader: Michelle Clark
Marketing manager: Catherine Slinn
Cover design: Stephanie Guyaz
Typeset by: C&M Digitals (P) Ltd, Chennai, India
Printed in India at Replika Press Pvt Ltd

© Phillip Chong Ho Shon 2015

First edition published 2012
Reprinted in 2012, three times in 2013 and three times in 2014.

Library of Congress Control Number: 2014959213

British Library Cataloguing in Publication data

A catalogue record for this book is available from the British Library

MIX
Paper from
responsible sources
FSC® C016779
www.fsc.org

ISBN 978-1-4739-1879-5
ISBN 978-1-4739-1880-1 (pbk)

At SAGE we take sustainability seriously. Most of our products are printed in the UK using FSC papers and boards. When we print overseas we ensure sustainable papers are used as measured by the Egmont grading system. We undertake an annual audit to monitor our sustainability.

To my wife, the MSG of my life

Contents

About the Author

Phillip Chong Ho Shon received his MA and PhD in criminal justice from the University of Illinois (Chicago); he also holds an MA in linguistics and a BA in philosophy from Northeastern Illinois University (Chicago). He is currently an associate professor of criminology at the University of Ontario Institute of Technology where he teaches courses in homicide, criminological theory, and integrating projects (capstone course). He is the author of *Language and Demeanor in Police–Citizen Encounters*, and *Respect, Defense, and Self-Identity: Profiling Parricide in Nineteenth-Century America, 1852–1899*. He is a co-editor (with Dragan Milovanovic) of *Serial Killers: Understanding Lust Murders*. For fun, he lifts weights and watches Asian gangster movies (not at the same time). He still has aspirations of becoming a professional wrestler and a long-haul trucker someday.

Acknowledgements

In another work, I stated that acknowledgements and citations are the currency with which intellectual debts are paid. Since then, I have made a small down payment, but now find that I have incurred additional debts. I am not sure if I can pay them back. This state of being in perpetual debt, it seems, is not atypical; rather, it is an unavoidable feature of life in the academy. Luckily, I happen to be surrounded by good people who do not mind being creditors. Here, again, I would like to thank those who have helped me shape the ideas in this book.

I am much indebted to Dr Brian Cutler for providing me with the initial impetus to write a book about this topic. Otherwise, this volume might not have materialized. Of course, recognizing potential in its nascent form is possible precisely because the ability to recognize good ideas in their nascent form has already been forged and refined from years of experience and unparalleled achievements as a distinguished scholar. I am grateful to Dr Steven Downing for reading and providing helpful comments and feedback on earlier drafts. I am also heavily indebted to Dr Kimberley Clow for providing obsessively helpful comments and feedback on several chapters; she also helped me to navigate the complexities and subtleties of psychology journal articles. To my aforementioned colleagues at the University of Ontario Institute of Technology, thank you. To my partner-in-crime 'Stonecold' Rick, thanks for the 'So what?' And to my most trusted friend, colleague, and confidant, CWW, thanks – for everything. You know who you are. I would like to thank Michael Carmichael at Sage for believing in my idea of the reading codes from the start. Without his support, this book would not exist. Finally, I would like to thank the anonymous reviewers for their helpful comments and suggestions. Whatever flaws remain in the book, however, they are my own.

Thanks to the students in Canada and at the University of Ontario Institute of Technology for being so receptive and open to the idea of the reading codes. I know it was painful reading with a ruler, a highlighter, and a pen. I understand. For their patience and understanding, I am grateful to the students in SSCI 4099U (Winter 2010, 2011) and SSCI 5020G (Fall 2010).

Although my teachers at Northeastern Illinois University will not – nor care to – remember me, I have not forgotten my professors who tried to teach me to be a critical thinker and a reader. I am quite certain that that was not an easy task, and I am not entirely sure that they succeeded. But the fault is mine. In particular, Dr Roger Gilman, Dr Sarah Hoagland, and Dr Stanley Kerr taught me to love and pursue wisdom for intrinsic ends. They may not know – and they may not even care – that they altered the course of my life, but I will now say what I could not have said twenty years ago: thank you for molding me into the form of a scholar. I am stumbling along, but hope to be able to walk on my own someday.

Dr Kerr passed away when I was away from Albany Park, Chicago. I didn't get a chance to say my final farewell. Dr Kerr, I want you to know that my heart still shakes when I read Nietzsche, and that I still cannot turn a page of *Will to Power* without thinking of you. *Let the world perish, but let there be philosophy, the philosopher, you.*

Phillip Chong Ho Shon

Introduction

Previous works that provide tips on how to successfully write research papers, theses, dissertations, and journal articles have emphasized that writing is like any other skill: it has to be developed, taught, and practiced daily (Cone & Foster, 2006; Glatthorn & Joyner, 2005; Miller, 2009; Rudestam & Newton, 2001; Silvia, 2007). Although graduate students are taught how to teach during their graduate education, through seminars and by working as teaching assistants, Silvia (2007, p. 6) laments that they are not taught how to write: 'the most common model of training is to presume that graduate students will learn about writing from their advisors.' The same argument could be made about reading.

In previous works, readers are taught how to structure their time to facilitate writing, how to outline their thoughts to prepare to write, how to structure a paper to submit to a journal, and how to conceptualize any 'action that is instrumental in completing a writing project' as writing (Silvia, 2007, p. 19). Professional academic writing, Paul Silvia argues, is a serious business that entails tremendous complexity, as the literature on a given topic must be extensively covered, data carefully analyzed, and the descriptions of research methods precisely worded (see Landrum, 2008; Noland, 1970). To do so, Silvia suggests, we may even have to read scientific journal articles we do not particularly like. The act of reading, again, is treated as a tertiary activity, necessarily subservient to and less consequential than writing.

This book is necessary because reading is often a blindly assumed and unexamined part of the writing process, for undergraduate and graduate students alike. If writing is learned throughout undergraduate and graduate education, as part of the honors thesis, master's thesis, PhD dissertation, and journal-article writing process, then, to my knowledge, no such formal and systematic training exists for reading in the social sciences; instead, students bring to universities – undergraduate and graduate – the reading habits and techniques they acquired in their formative years in primary/elementary schooling. Unlike philosophy and literary criticism, where careful reading is taught to students at the undergraduate and graduate level, disciplines in the social sciences tacitly expect students to already be competent readers.

With such an unexamined assumption in place, it is not surprising that advanced undergraduates (third- and fourth-year students in institutions of higher education), and graduate students have trouble reading critically in order to write their undergraduate research papers, honors theses, and graduate-level texts. Rather than assuming that students already possess the skills necessary to be critical readers, this book teaches students – advanced undergraduate students writing research papers and honors theses, and graduate students writing theses and dissertations – how to read so that they are able to maximize their output in the writing process. Reading critically is an essential skill at all levels of instruction at university.

This book illuminates the steps in the prewriting process that scholars in the field have uncritically presupposed in the practice (not theory) of writing and reading. For example, I am sure that students, at one time or another throughout their career, have heard the directive, 'You have to read critically' from their professors. The problem with that benign advice is that telling someone to do something is meaningless unless how to do that something is actually taught. The numerous how-to books on the market do little better. That is, in such books, readers are given general and vague instructions on how to read critically; they are told that a good critique of the literature is developed from 'careful readings.' Others advise that readers need to maintain a 'critical perspective.' The problem common to all such benign prescriptions is that only a few have explicitly unpacked what it means to read 'critically.'

Sometimes, the directive to be 'critical' seems elusive and unduly complex at times and elegantly simple in others. For example, Wallace and Wray (2011, p. 29) state that a crucial skill involved in critical reading entails 'identifying authors' underlying aims and agendas so that you can take them into account in your evaluation of the text in hand.' Critical reading, according to Wallace and Wray, means discerning the main claims, as well as hidden ones, of one's readings. Such reading is done with an eye toward identifying gaps that exist in the literature, and as a way of preparing one's own paper. Cottrell (2011) echoes a similar point, arguing that critical reading involves analyzing, reflecting, evaluating, and judging a text's merits. She further posits that critical reading is a logical extension of critical thinking which includes paying 'attention to detail, identifying patterns and trends ... taking different perspectives, and considering implications and distant consequences' (p. 5). That is, Wallace and Wray (2011) and Cottrell (2011) tacitly suggest that reading occurs on numerous levels, and involves completing several tasks at once. Reading in an academic context is neither easy nor simple. As a way of keeping track of one's ideas that arise during reading, some scholars advise creating mental maps or asking questions.

2

Or, if maps are provided, the directions are too vague or unwieldy to be effective. For example, there are two well-known reading strategies that prior scholars have noted: the EEECA model and the SQ3R model. In the first, readers are taught to Examine, Evaluate, Establish, Compare, and Argue (EEECA) so that new claims can be developed (see Jesson, Matheson, & Lacey, 2011, p. 48). In the second, readers are taught first to survey, skim, and scan the readings, to question if the readings are relevant to a student's aims, and then to 'read the text carefully … recall the main points … and review the text to confirm' (Ridley, 2012, p. 64). These traditional methods of reading are just a bit better than the vague directions that are often provided by instructors.

According to others who have written on this topic, 'critical' reading is important because it allows readers to develop new ideas, claims, and unique 'spins' if they don't have new ideas of their own. Research articles in social science journals, however, are necessarily full of new and yet-to-be-developed ideas. A gap or a deficiency in the literature – absence of new ideas – is the reason why scholars write journal articles; that is why authors discuss limitations of their research and recommendations for future works in the papers they are writing – as a tacit way of setting up the work they will do in the future or of providing an itinerary for others who may want to remedy that gap in the literature. Simply put, critiques are embedded in bits and pieces in journal articles; readers just have to be taught how to decipher them in the text. Writers have difficulty developing new ideas because they have not learned the art of textual criticism and critical reading – not because new ideas do not exist. Using my reading codes (see Figure 1), this book teaches students how to approach social science journal articles as texts that can be deciphered structurally, mechanically, and grammatically. This book thus fills in the content of general advice, such as 'read critically,' by teaching students the techniques of critical reading.

Another significant problem that is not adequately addressed in previous work is one of management. Let's suppose that an honors thesis student or a beginning graduate student is writing a thesis on a chosen topic, and has identified 50 peer-reviewed journal articles that have been published within the past 15 years. Is there a way to read the articles that will enhance the writing process by organizing the themes and patterns in the literature as well as their critiques? Most how-to books recommend the use of 3×5 index cards as a way of organizing and collating relevant information to be used during the reading, outlining, and writing process. To be able to even come up with a rough outline, however, the student will have to have digested and organized the readings in a particular way; and unless that student sat down with a blank sheet of paper and kept track of recurring themes, patterns, and gaps in the literature, the critique of the literature that should have emerged is apt to get lost in the unstructured reading.

For example, consider the 'concise critical notes' form that students are advised to fill out when reading articles and papers (see Cottrell, 2011, p. 157). It is similar to the 3×5 index card method in that the form contains slots for bibliographic information. However, in addition, there are nine sections that contain a total of 13 questions that need to be answered to use the form effectively (e.g., 'What is the paper setting out to prove? How does it advance our understanding of the subject?'). Similarly, Wallace and Wray's (2011) 'critical analysis of a text' form has ten questions that readers should answer after they have completed their reading of a text; those ten questions contain an additional 26 questions that need to be answered in order to complete the form – a total of 36 questions. Some of those questions include, 'What type of literature is this? What is being claimed that is relevant to answering my question? ... and To what extent are claims supported or challenged by others' works?' (pp. 237–46).

Answering the questions that Cottrell (2011) and Wallace and Wray (2011) pose in their respective forms would indeed constitute a critical engagement with one's reading, as the answers would, essentially, enable readers to see recurring themes in their readings, as well as potential criticisms that they could develop to use in their own papers. However, the sheer number of questions, as well as the form of the answers, fails to provide the structure and constraint needed to maximize their utility. Simply put, rather than expecting readers to fill out answers in extended narrative form, a code-based system of note-taking would provide the constraint needed to organize the responses to those questions. A code-based system would be much more effective for the following reasons.

1. The responses would be based on the textual function of the articles that are being read.
2. Students would be able to synthesize their ideas more effectively because they would receive adequate practice in reducing and condensing complex ideas and sentences into one to two key words (thematic codes).
3. Those key words would facilitate visual inspection and easy retrieval. Repetition of recurring themes in results and summaries would be easier to identify using one to two words rather than lengthy sentences.

The reading code sheet that I have developed systematizes the reading, note-taking, and organizing of voluminous amounts of information in an easily identifiable and retrievable format. It is my contention that previous works on reading and writing are inadequate because the two acts are treated separately. As I see it, they ought to be treated similarly. The method of managing information gleaned from the readings that I am advocating in this book (Reading Code Organization Sheet or RCOS) is not new or novel. In fact, the form of RCOS is portended in other well-regarded works. For example, Machi and McEvoy (2012) discuss how to use their Literature Review Tally

FIGURE 1 Dr Phil's reading codes for an RCOS for social science journal articles

Code location in text	Code	Meaning
Introduction/ Literature Review	WTD	**What They Do**: what the author(s) purport to do in a paper/book; this code captures the main research question that the author is posing in the text.
Literature Review	SPL	**Summary of Previous Literature**: this sentence, paragraph, or page describes a simple summary of the results from prior studies. This process entails a tremendous amount of condensation, taking complex ideas and reducing them into paragraphs, sentences, and if the author is brilliant, one word.
Literature Review	CPL	**Critique of Previous Literature**: the author is providing a critique and a description of the limitations of the previous and existing scholarly works. CPL is conceptually related to POC, GAP, and SPL since the deficiencies in the existing works provide a theoretical, methodological, and analytical justification as to why the current work is warranted. CPL usually follows SPL since the author has to first proffer a body of ideas before it can be criticized.
Literature Review	GAP	**Gap**: the author is (probably in some systematic way) pointing out the missing elements in current literature. When GAP and CPL are done properly, a reader should be able to anticipate the RAT even before the author declares it.
Literature Review/ Introduction	RAT	**Rationale**: the author is providing the justification of why the work is necessary and warranted. RAT should be deduced and logically follow if the author has CPLed and GAPed previous literature.
Results/Discussion	ROF	**Results of Findings**: describes the primary results of the current article. This code is usually found in the abstract, results section, and conclusion since this point must be hammered at least three times in most social scientific journals.
Discussion	RCL	**Results Consistent with Literature**: describes the findings of the current work that are consistent with the existing literature. That is, the author's own work supports the work that others have done.
Discussion	RTC	**Results To the Contrary**: describes the findings of the current work that are inconsistent with the existing literature. That is, the author's own work does not support the work that others have done.

(Continued)

FIGURE 1 (Continued)

Code location in text	Code	Meaning
Conclusion	WTDD	**What They Did**: what the author(s) have done in a paper/book; a logical and sequential cognate of WTD. This code captures the main research question that the author has answered and contributed to the body of literature on the chosen topic.
Conclusion	RFW	**Recommendations for Future Works**: the current work is not complete; the author is providing a map of what is still lacking (GAP) in the literature and recommending that others do in future work.
Reading Strategies		
	POC	**Point of Critique**: a deficiency in the current article or literature that *you* (the student author) could critique and exploit as a way of remedying the gap in the literature for a future paper.
	MOP	**Missed an Obvious Point**: the author that you are reading has missed an obvious theoretical, conceptual, and analytical connection to earlier works. (MOP usually occurs when the article's author has not read sufficiently or widely.)
	RPP	**Relevant Point to Pursue**: and to mine in another paper. Although this code does not point out any limitations and gaps in the current work, the stated point could be used as a POC in a future paper. Obviously, RPP entails MOP and GAP.
	WIL	Will this theoretical and conceptual connection be logically teased out to its conclusion to reconcile a text that is fraught with tension and needs resolving?

Matrix (LRTM). Jesson, Matheson, and Lacey (2011) argue for the effectiveness of visual note-making systems such as mind maps and column-based presentation of notes. Ridley (2012) also discusses the value of a tabular form of note organization. In that sense, RCOS only extends the general strategies that previous scholars have already noted. It differs because the reading codes organize the information in a more effective way than other reading and information management techniques.

There are other books that teach students how to understand and digest existing research. Most of the how-to books in academia, with the possible exception of Paul Silvia's (2007) *How to Write a Lot* and Scott Harris's (2014) *How to Critique Journal Articles in the Social Sciences*, suffer from a major shortcoming: they are unwieldy. For example, *Reading and Understanding Research* (Locke, Silverman, & Spirduso, 2010) is 312 pages long; *How to Write a Master's Thesis* (Bui, 2009) is 320 pages; *Surviving Your Dissertation: A Comprehensive Guide to Content and Process* (Rudestam, 2007) is 328 pages; even *Conducting Research Literature Reviews: From the Internet to Paper* (Fink, 2010) is a whopping 272 pages. A book that teaches students how to read cannot be long and cumbersome; it needs to be succinct, concise, and operational – not long-winded and theoretical. *How to Read Journal Articles in the Social Sciences* meets that goal.

This book is directed at upper-level undergraduates and graduate students. This book's primary aim is to be used as a supplementary text that undergraduate honors thesis supervisors and directors of teaching and learning centers in colleges and universities can recommend to their students, and as a supplementary text in first-year professional seminars for graduate students. *How to Read Journal Articles in the Social Sciences* will be relevant and helpful in preparing their students to write original research papers, advanced literature reviews, and theoretically oriented essays in undergraduate writing courses and research methods courses as well. It is my contention that reading critically is a necessary part of undergraduate and graduate education.

A book like *How to Read Journal Articles in the Social Sciences* will be particularly useful as preparatory reading material for international students who are preparing to go abroad to North America, the United Kingdom, and Australia for their studies, particularly students from Asia. First, China, India, and Korea contribute the largest share of international students who come to North America for undergraduate and graduate education. Second, even native speakers of English experience difficulty reading and writing social science texts when they enter upper-level courses in their undergraduate curriculum and graduate school. That is because they have not been taught how to do so.

International students who speak English as a second language therefore have to shoulder a double burden: (1) they have to acquire sociolinguistic competence as second language speakers in order to function in their new social milieu; (2) they have to acquire vocabulary competence in their respective disciplines and in academic writing. Rather than trying to comprehend and act on vague instructions from their professors and thesis advisors about 'reading critically' and 'synthesizing the literature' during the writing process, my book will teach students how to read so that they can organize information during their reading to be able to write more effectively. Being prepared to read critically during their studies will help international students overcome burden (2) before they encounter it. Of course, a similar point can be made about native speakers of English, too.

A Note on Terminology

A few explanations are in order regarding the terminology that will be used to describe the various institutions of higher learning throughout this book. I do so to eliminate any potential confusion that may arise in readers. For example, 'high schools' and 'secondary schools' refers to schooling that precedes higher education in North America (the US, Canada). In countries such as Sweden, Norway, and Finland, these schools are known as upper secondary schools. Such distinctions apply to institutions of higher education as well. Again, as an example, schooling that occurs after high school in the US is collectively referred to as 'community colleges.' Community colleges are two-year institutions where vocational and technical trades are primarily taught. They are also institutions some students attend prior to enrolling in a four-year college or university as a way of defraying the burgeoning cost of a university education. Community colleges in Canada are known simply as 'college.' In Australia, these types of institutions are known as 'technical colleges,' in Finland, 'vocational schools,' in the UK, 'further education.' While the names differ, the function of these types of institutions is similar across countries.

Colleges and universities in an American sense are known as 'university' in Canada, and higher education (HE) in the UK, Sweden, and Australia; in Finland, they are referred to as bachelors' programs. Despite the different names, their functions are similar. The emphasis on higher education and learning, as I see it, is still imbued with that original Aristotelian spirit; not much has changed I think. Students go to a university to profess their ignorance and to learn something new. Students do not go to a university to confirm the beliefs they already hold. When I use the term 'college' or 'university,' I am referring to four-year institutions of higher education rather than the technical and vocational schools and community colleges. The term 'undergraduates' refers to students who are enrolled in four-year institutions of higher education.

Similarly, when I use the term 'graduate education,' I am referring to schooling that occurs after the completion of a four-year degree (e.g., master's degree, PhD degree). I refer to students in the master's and PhD programs as 'graduate students.' That I refer to four-year institutions of higher learning as colleges and universities, and students in those institutions as undergraduates, reflects my American roots more than anything. I apologize to readers who may find my American sensibilities a bit obtuse. But as one famous cultural figure (Popeye) once claimed, 'I yam what I yam and that's all I yam.'

This distinction between names that are used to describe the institutions of higher education is also meaningful in another way. It is implicative for the type of written work that is carried out in the completion of those degrees. For example, a dissertation in a North American context refers to a very specific type of document that is reserved for doctoral (PhD) students. A dissertation is the culminating text that PhD students must complete in order to be awarded their degrees. It is not applicable to master's students or undergraduates. In the UK, however, the term dissertation is used in a broader sense. In this book, I use the term dissertation to refer to the projects that are restricted to PhD students. The term 'thesis' requires an additional explanation.

'Thesis' is used in two ways to describe the document that graduates and undergraduates submit in order to complete their degrees. For example, a master's degree is usually a two-year program of study in the US and Canada. Master's students generally complete a thesis in order to meet the requirements of that degree. Although a master's thesis requires original data collection and analysis of some sort, thereby making it empirical, some students write conceptual and theoretical pieces that are not empirical. Similarly, upper-level undergraduates (third- and fourth-year students in a four-year university) who are talented and bright undertake an honors thesis. In the US, honors theses are written by students who are part of an honors college/program, distinct from the general university curriculum. An honors thesis involves a two-semester sequence of study where a literature review and a proposal defense occur in the first semester, and data collection, analysis, and several drafts before completion in the second. In Canada, honors (honours) theses are written by students who must apply and be accepted by their respective programs in order to undertake such a project: it also requires a two-semester sequence of study. An undergraduate honors thesis is very similar to a master's thesis in that it requires original data collection and analysis. Both are demanding and require quite a bit of work. While the names used to designate such projects may differ across countries, the function of these types of documents is very similar: production of an original and creative claim/argument/finding of some sort.

There are a host of other terms that are used to describe the numerous types of writing assignments that are given to students in colleges and universities: essays, position papers, reflection papers, term papers, literature reviews, annotated bibliographies, and research papers, just to name a few. A 'research paper' generally is assigned in third- and fourth-year courses to get students to critically evaluate a topic, and produce a new claim and argument of sorts. It is used as a general term to encapsulate writing projects that require synthesis and critique of the literature along with the production of an original argument and/or claim (Wallace & Wray, 2011). A research paper may or may not require empirical aspects. Capstone projects refer to the papers that undergraduates are required to complete in their fourth year in a university. The name given to this paper and project also varies by institution in North America: they are sometimes known as 'writing intensive' or 'writing in the discipline' courses. My current institution calls them 'integrating projects,' for students are expected to integrate their previous coursework and knowledge into an original, final paper. The names differ, but the function is the same. I will use the term 'research paper' to refer to original papers that undergraduates have to write which are non-theses.

Finally, one more qualification is needed on address terms used in this book. Students, sometimes, are not sure what to call their teachers in colleges and universities. I remember how annoyed I became when my students in Louisiana called me 'Mr Phil.' I later learned that appending the title 'Mr' was a way that students signaled deference, especially to people they liked. The annoying address term did not seem so annoying after I learned that lesson. I was flattered. When I finished my PhD, students changed the title from Mr to Dr and started calling me Dr Phil. That appellation has since stuck.

'Dr' is a title that is conferred by a terminal degree-granting institution. One earns that title by completing the requirements for a PhD and writing and successfully defending a dissertation. I could become homeless next year and live on the street, but no one can take that title away from me. It's mine. I earned it. Period. The title 'professor,' however, is a position that an institution of higher education confers on a person who is hired to teach for them – at least in a North American context. In Europe and the UK, that title means something far more prestigious, and is not used lightly. If I am no longer teaching at a university, I am no longer a professor, so the title does not apply. In this book, I use the term 'professor' to indicate someone who appears in front of a university class and teaches. Again, while the name and meaning used to designate such a figure differs by country and convention, the work done is similar. I use the term professor and teacher interchangeably throughout this book.

Organization of the Book

Chapter 1: The Challenges of Reading. This chapter begins by examining the previous models of reading that have attempted to teach the techniques of critical reading, and discusses one of the main limitations students face when trying to implement such techniques. The challenges of reading on multiple levels are discussed. The readers are then introduced to the reading codes in the context of social science journal articles. This chapter explains why students need to get their primary information about the topics they have selected for their papers from reputable journals rather than other sources.

Chapter 2: Trying to Fix Mechanical and Structural Writing Problems with Abstract Tools. This chapter begins with one of the most perplexing and mysterious aspects of paper writing in colleges and universities: how professors arrive at the grades they assign to students' papers. In this chapter, I describe the necessity of and the origins of the grading code sheet that preceded the Reading Code Organization Sheet. I relate the failures I encountered trying to teach students how to write research papers and theses using the grading code sheet.

Chapter 3: Should I Even Read This? How to Read the Abstract, General Introduction, and Methods Sections. This chapter teaches students how they ought to read the abstract, the introduction, and the methods sections using the reading codes. By teaching how to read the abstract, this chapter attempts to show students how to mine for the pertinent information necessary to determine if an article should be included in one's literature review without actually reading the entire paper. By learning how to critically read introductions, the practice of anticipatory reading is demonstrated, whereby students use the elements contained in the introduction to rehearse and anticipate the shape of the more complex arguments to emerge in the rest of the text. Students are also taught how to use one particular reading code, Point of Critique (POC), in their reading of the data and methods section to cultivate a methodological critique of previous studies along with a rationale for their own proposed works.

Chapter 4: So What? How to Read the General Literature Review, Psychology Introductions, and Results Sections. This chapter teaches students how they ought to read the literature review using the reading codes. Students will learn the rudiments of structural and grammar-based reading to anticipate emergent critiques, hypothesis generation, and rationale for a study – hence answering the 'So what?' question. Students are also taught how to make the transition from the act of reading the results (ROF) section to organizing summaries (SPL) as part of their own writing process.

Chapter 5: Becoming a Part of the Scholarly Community: How to Read the Discussion and Conclusion. This chapter teaches students how they ought to read the discussion and conclusion using the reading codes. Students will learn how key words in both these sections of journal articles tether our work to those of previous researchers.

Chapter 6: Highlighting and Organizing the ROF, SPL, CPL, GAP, RFW, and POC. This chapter proffers practical tips for using the accoutrements of reading: ruler, pen, and highlighter. I demonstrate how these essential tools of reading are to be used to slow down the act of reading and to 'do' the act of critical reading that others have advised but never taught. In addition to reading, this chapter provides concrete suggestions about how to organize the information gathered through the reading codes to maximize organization, management, and retrieval of information necessary for paper writing. After students are introduced to the Reading Code Organization Sheet (RCOS) as a way of collecting, organizing, and managing information, they are taught how to create an outline using the RCOS before writing that first professional-quality research paper.

Chapter 7: Will the Reading Organization Code Sheet Work on Non-social Science Texts? This chapter tests the applicability of the RCOS to non-social science texts. In particular, classic philosophical works are used as examples to determine the generalizability of the RCOS to book-length texts and journal articles in philosophy – arguably, one of the more abstract and abstruse disciplines in academia. This chapter argues that the ideas foundational to the reading codes are applicable across various types of academic texts and disciplines.

Chapter 8: Concluding Remarks. This chapter argues that reading and writing are inextricably related acts. That is, despite the solitary character of both academic activities, they are fundamentally social and intersubjective acts, inaugurating readers and writers into the socio-moral order of the scholarly community.

1

The Challenges of Reading

Professors often tell their students to read carefully and critically. Students may then valiantly attempt to translate that benign advice into practice: they highlight blocks of text, sometimes entire pages, and try to answer those numerous questions that previous scholars have recommended that they ask themselves as a way of engaging with the text: What is the author's main argument? What evidence does the author provide to support her claims? What presuppositions does the author make in order to make his ideas work, etc. (Cottrell, 2011). In attempting to be critical, I have noticed that students get bogged down. Moreover, readings in social science texts – books and articles – are challenging in another way if the subject of the readings is unrelated to a student's area of interest. That is to say, there are many factors that interfere with a student's ability to read in general and read critically in particular. Telling students to go read critically is different from teaching them how to read critically. To do the latter, students need to be shown what critical reading is and how it differs from ordinary reading – reading a novel on a breezy Sunday afternoon.

Students also do not have good reading habits. Although smartphones and tablets have enabled students to become connected with their peers and the world through various social media outlets, especially within the past ten years or so, they have provided an easy means to become disconnected from the text and the author through incessant distractions. Students will be listening to a lecture, answer a text message or a Facebook post, and then return to their lecture. They attempt to read an article for class, but stop midway to answer an instant message, text, or some other request for further communication. Those types of repeated interruptions do not make for careful readings that require full concentration. There are other challenges that arise while reading.

There are several models that attempt to teach students the techniques of careful reading. Two well-known techniques that are used to teach reading to college and university students are the SQ3R model and the EEECA model. The first method, SQ3R, purports to teach students to read 'efficiently' and to engage with the text in active ways (Ridley, 2012, p. 64).

1. **S**urvey the text to ascertain the gist or general idea.
2. **Q**uestion – while surveying the text, think about questions that you would like the text to answer if you decide it is relevant to read in more detail.
3. **R**ead the text carefully if you think it is pertinent for your research.
4. **R**ecall the main points after you have read the text.
5. **R**eview the text to confirm that you have recalled all the main points that are significant for you and your work.

Readers are first instructed to skim and scan to determine if a piece of text should be read further – to discern whether a piece of text ought to be included in one's careful reading. Once a 'yes' decision has been reached, students are instructed to 'read and make connections with other texts' as a way of enhancing recall. Readers are then told to recall and review the text after a 'manageable' chunk has been read by writing sentence summaries. The SQ3R method of reading begins with five directives to keep in mind as the reading begins. But in addition to the preceding five directives, students are told that reading critically and analytically entails more questions and steps that ought to be considered (Ridley, 2012, p. 66).

1. What is the author's central argument or main point, i.e. what does the author want you, the reader, to accept?
2. What conclusions does the author reach?
3. What evidence does the author put forward in support of his or her argument and conclusions?
4. Do you think the evidence is strong enough to support the arguments and conclusions, i.e. is the evidence relevant and wide reaching enough?
5. Does the author make any unstated assumptions about shared beliefs with the readers?
6. Can these assumptions be challenged?
7. What is the background context in which the text was written? Does the cultural and historical context have an effect on the author's assumptions, the content and the way it has been presented?

These questions that a student should ask during reading are absolutely correct. Readers should pay attention to the main points, evidence that supports an argument, the hidden assumptions behind the text, as well as the historical and cultural factors that may illuminate the contexts behind the text's production. If readers can keep all of the aforementioned points in mind as they are reading, the questions would uncover an author's main points as well as the assumptions that she makes about the topic she is writing about.

In this spirit, the SQ3R model is consistent with the EEECA model that is also widely used (Jesson, Matheson, & Lacey, 2011, p. 48).

1. **E**xamine or analyze the topic – try to examine it from more than one perspective.
2. **E**valuate or critique the topic, thereby making a judgment about it.
3. **E**stablish relationships and show how they are related.
4. **C**ompare and contrast the ideas – are they similar to other work or how do they differ from other work?
5. **A**rgue for or against something to try to persuade the reader to agree.

Both methods attempt to have their readers identify the relevance and suitability of the texts that they have selected for their academic writing projects. Both methods attempt to teach readers to be critical by asking pertinent questions during the reading process; both methods also attempt to get readers to develop a critique of previous literature on some grounds. In this sense, both models work quite well; they do what they are meant to do. If students can keep all those questions in mind as they are reading and then go on to answer them, they will have read academic texts in ways that were intended. However, the two methods do not differ significantly from the advice that other writers have already recommended. For example, Cone and Foster (2006) instruct their readers to be critical by keeping a record of observations while reading in order to arrive at a major insight about a topic based on those observations. Rudestam and Newton (2001) offer a list of questions to keep in mind while reading as a way of cultivating critique and structuring reading – all 21 of them.

The difficulty with the SQ3R and EEECA models, as well as previous writers who have instructed students to be critical readers, is that the benign advice is difficult to implement and execute. As noted, Rudestam and Newton's (2001) list of questions to keep in mind as students read would translate into 21 questions that they would have to recall and answer. Similarly, the SQ3R would translate into 12 questions that readers would have to keep in mind during the act of reading. The difficulty so far with the existing reading models is compounded when the next step in the reading process is taken into consideration. The challenge arises when readers keep a list of the unwieldy questions, and then attempt to answer them. The answers would vary from one sentence to several sentences, thereby lacking consistency, succinctness, and precision.

The absence of a systematic and consistent coding system that captures the general structure of the answers would also hinder the retrieval of pertinent information – a palpable challenge, as each sentence would have to be reviewed individually rather than through casual inspection and identification. An effective reading method, therefore, should be complemented by an organization system that facilitates easy retrieval. The organizational system should be primarily visual – advice that is consistent with what others have reported (Jesson, Matheson, & Lacey, 2011; Machi & McEvoy, 2012; Ridley, 2012). The notes that result from one's readings should be organized into visual – tabular – forms; tabular notes in the form of codes should expedite information retrieval, which then makes writing easier. Reading, writing, information storage and retrieval are all related components of the reading and writing – learning – process.

The reading codes that have been developed for this book are generally applicable to most social science journal articles, although I have found that the codes can be used in humanities journal articles and books too. Furthermore, the reading codes are organized and occur in such a way that readers can anticipate and predict the occurrence of certain codes at expectable locations, thereby structuring the reading process along the contours already delineated by the writing conventions of the social sciences. The reading codes usurp that pre-existing convention. For example, the codes RCL, RTC, WTDD, and RFW generally appear in discussion and conclusion sections; they do not appear in introductions and literature review and methods sections. Similarly, the codes SPL, CPL, GAP, and RAT generally appear in the literature review sections, although they tend to be repeated in the abstract, introduction, and the literature reviews in condensed forms. The use of the reading codes thus reduces the words needed to describe the functions of a block of text. The codes also facilitate visual inspection.

The reading strategy codes entail a bit more sophistication and practice. For example, the code WIL is a very advanced reading technique. Just from reading a question posed in the text or a sentence that is embedded in it, the reader 'sees' all the connections that will need to be made in order for a position or an argument to work, and asks if these connections will be teased out. When I took a course with a renowned literary critic, he would always identify sentences and questions that would, in essence, contain the hidden premises presupposed in a text to make a body of ideas work, which would then be supported in an author's argument or become unraveled in subsequent analysis due to the tension and inconsistency embedded in the author's logic and text. The literary critic would find those make-it-or-break-it sentences and ask the WIL question.

It was always awesome to see that literary critic read, interpret, and analyze a piece of text, whether that text was authored by Isaiah Berlin, John Stuart Mill, Immanuel Kant, Thomas Hobbes, or John Rawls. The code WIL emerged from seeing that teacher's advanced reading techniques. I rarely find myself using the WIL code because: (1) I am not that widely read; (2) I am not that smart; (3) I can rarely see beyond the myopic confines of my own discipline. To use the WIL code, the reader has to be at least three steps ahead of the author. Only talented scholars/readers are capable of such feats. Although it is entirely possible that an exceptional undergraduate or graduate student has read extensively and can challenge the assumptions upon which a work rests, the move is a very unlikely one.

Along similar lines, a reader would have to be well and widely read, and be familiar with the literature on a topic in order to see that an obvious point has been missed (MOP: Missed an Obvious Point). That is, a connection that should have been made by the author was not made – for whatever reason: perhaps the author has not read a key book or article in the field that she should have read; perhaps the author forgot to cite and mention an important scholar and his/her body of ideas that should have been discussed; or perhaps for some reason the author is simply slighting another scholar and deliberately omitting him/her from the paper. But the point is that those missed points ought not to have been missed, hence, MOP – missed an obvious point. Those obvious points that have been missed can be mined by students and pursued in another paper, for it is a Relevant Point to Pursue (RPP). Or the student may read something that could become a Point of Critique (POC), which could be used as a basis for a critique of previous literature (CPL). The codes POC, MOP, and RPP necessitate that the readers 'see' and understand the findings of the study that is currently being read and connect it to the broader literature – or make a connection to a topic and literature that one would not ordinarily expect. Making those unexpected and unforeseen connections is what leads to an original and creative claim. Of course, without adequate background reading, it is difficult to make those connections.

In the context of social science scholarship, there is one fundamental task that falls on the shoulders of readers: on what grounds will you – the student reader – critique the literature on a topic that you have selected? Will you be able to read through the vast literature on a topic you have selected (e.g., school climate research, undergraduate mentoring programs, juvenile homicide, news coverage of crime, women's health) and develop a Critique of Previous Literature (CPL), which logically leads to a shortcoming (GAP)? From this critique that you have developed, you, the student, should be able to propose a way to remedy that very GAP you have identified.

For example, you may read through 30, 40, or 50 journal articles and come to the conclusion that previous works have carried out only cross-sectional studies of your subject population rather than longitudinal ones. Or you may notice that previous works use a very limited sample in their studies. Both criticisms, for most social science journal articles, may be valid. Students may be right to note that previous studies failed to include adequate samples or conduct a longitudinal examination of subjects. If one of these critiques is the ground upon which you the student are critiquing the previous literature (CPL), then will you remedy those very GAPs that you have identified?

17

You may very well have the analytical skills, data support services, and the will to undertake such a project. However, if you do not, then you do not have the means to rectify that shortcoming that exists in the literature. You have correctly identified a shortcoming, but it may not be appropriate for you. It may be much more realistic and pragmatic for you to identify shortcomings in the literature that you can remedy without thinking yourself into an anxiety-riddled panic attack or crumbling under the sheer magnitude of your ambitious plans.

The CPL you develop should inform the research question that you ask and answer in your paper – whether that paper is a fourth-year capstone project, honors thesis, master's thesis, or a PhD dissertation. The type of paper that you are writing varies according to the text's requirements and the project's scale and sophistication. However, the underlying form and logic of the social science articles, and the shortcomings that must be identified to justify one's project, which leads to the formulation of research questions and the project's successful resolution are similar for undergraduate- and graduate-level projects. Previous literature can always be critiqued on numerous grounds (Harris, 2014). The type of critique that is developed differs by scale, scope, and the sophistication of the student reader. The logic of the criticism remains the same: criticisms are fundamentally based on a negation – on what has not been done in the literature.

Reading also occurs on multiple levels. Rushing through the texts as if one is practicing speed-reading will not contribute to critical reading; one is apt to miss important points through such a type of reading. For example, when reading social science journal articles, the coding of the function of the texts should occur in the right margin where feasible (i.e., SPL, CPL, RAT, RCL, etc.). If a sentence, paragraph, or page provides a summary, a critique, rationale, or results, those codes should also be written in the right margin where feasible. This task is the first step in critical reading. When reading the literature reviews, methods, and results sections, thematic code insertions should be done in the left margins. That is, each paragraph should be distilled to one or two words that capture the essence of what that paragraph is about. That reduction and condensation will help organize the student's own literature review as similar themes are noticed. This second step in being critical entails condensing complex ideas and words into one to two words that can be thematically organized and recalled later.

Once social science texts are coded along the preceding lines, students should be able to see the qualitative differences between social science journal articles. For example, students will begin to notice that a well-written paper provides a well-crafted rationale (RAT) for why the paper and the topic that the authors have selected are important and worth doing, while not-so-well written journal articles neglect to tell readers the significance and importance of their work. Students will begin to see that some authors fail to synthesize the literature in thematic ways, instead, discussing only one author throughout the course of a paragraph. Students should also be paying attention to the way sentences are syntactically, mechanically, and grammatically organized as well, for they will see differences from author to author. They will notice that some social science authors make elementary errors while others go to great lengths to craft beautifully written sentences. Once the preceding points are clarified, a reader can then go on to question hidden assumptions, the cultural and historical context of a text's production, etc. Reading occurs on numerous levels and students should be treating the texts they are reading as a detective would comb through evidence at a crime scene. Every piece of evidence – paragraph, sentence, punctuation – is important, for it illuminates something about the author.

Although cheating in academia has been discussed in assorted ways, from cheating on tests to plagiarizing a paper, rarely do educators talk about cheating that occurs during reading. How so, you ask? As I have explained in this chapter and will demonstrate in later chapters, reading is a complex task that requires one's undivided attention. Reading is also a moral act. Reading social science journal articles involves reading through all sections, from the abstract and introduction to the methods, results, discussion, and the conclusion, for the type of information that is available in each section will be invaluable later. However, students do not read the full text. Somewhere during their university education process, they learned – someone told them – that they only needed to read the introduction and the conclusion to 'know what the article is about.' That practice is a disingenuous act of a student and a scholar. Taking those kinds of shortcuts are insincere and unfaithful acts of a scholar. That disingenuous spirit transmits into writing as well, for some students cite authors and articles they have not even read. Those acts constitute academic dishonesty and fraud, for students are claiming to have done something that they have not. I cannot claim to have climbed Mt Everest when I have not. Doing so would mean deception.

When students cite authors they have not read, they are misrepresenting their work and themselves. Just as morality figures in important ways in the production of written academic work, it also plays an important part in the reading process. That a theft has not been discovered and that the thief has not been caught does not mean that a crime has not occurred. That theft may not exist in official records but it exists in two places. It would exist in the all-perceiving mind of God, according to Bishop George Berkeley. It would also reside in the heart of the offender. It would also exist in a third place. If an instructor has read the work that the said student cited but has not read, then she too would know. If such self-deception were to persist in school work (and in life), there are bound to be psychic consequences, at least according to some psychotherapists (Horney, 1950). Students may not see themselves as scholars; they may not even want to. However, when they are enrolled in a university, they become scholars during their tenure there, and ought to at least emulate the proper attitude and practices of a scholar: they should approach their texts with humility, and report their findings truthfully and faithfully.

So what are the types of texts that exist in academia? There are numerous types of publications, from books and monographs to book reviews, review essays, theoretical treatises, literature reviews, research notes, and commentaries (see Harris, 2014). For our purposes, however, we are concerned with one particular type of text – the social science journal article. Why make such a fuss about journal articles? Because a published journal article is the gold standard in the social sciences. It is the currency of academic life and business. While there are several types of social science journal articles, the ones that involve original claims tend to fall into two predominant types: empirical articles and theoretical/conceptual treatises. In the first, scholars collect and analyze data, in both quantitative and qualitative forms, and then write up the results of their studies. In the second, scholars use the work that others have already produced and use previous claims to critique and produce a unique claim of their own. Journal articles are important because that is where the cutting-edge research and findings will first appear. Innovative claims and ideas usually appear first in journal articles – in empirical or theoretical form.

As others have already described, journal articles undergo a blind peer review process before they are published. For example, when I submit a paper to a journal, it is usually reviewed by three other experts. Those three reviewers must agree that my paper makes a meaningful contribution to the literature and knowledge before they decide to publish it. If my paper is shoddy, it will be rejected (as it often is). Hence, papers that appear in peer-reviewed publications have already undergone a fairly thorough vetting process. That is why journal articles are considered the gold standard. Usually, the words '*Journal of ...*' or '*... Review*' in the journal title are good indicators that you are reading a peer-reviewed journal. Each social science discipline has its top-tiered journals. When students are writing papers of any kind for their classes, they should be reading through journal articles. Let me illustrate the importance of using journal articles as a reputable source for writing one's paper.

For the past several years, I have taught a course on homicide. Every semester, students always and inevitably write about serial killers. Female, undergraduate English majors in particular love them: they can't get enough of Ted 'the necrophiliac' Bundy, Gary 'Green River' Ridgeway, Jeffrey 'the cannibal' Dahmer, Jack the Ripper, and others like them. When asked to describe the papers they wrote on serial killers, those students would usually name their favorite serial killer, much like the way any Canadian male could name a favorite hockey player or a true Chicagoan can name a favorite player from the 1985 Chicago Bears; and then they would describe the true-crime books that they had read (usually written by a retired FBI agent), and how the killers' poor and miserable childhoods spent at the hands of domineering mothers had 'caused' their violent propensities. I would then ask, 'Well, how did your paper contribute to the literature on serial homicides?' 'What do you mean?' students would ask. 'I mean, does your work on serial murder support or refute existing research on serial killers? If your findings on or understanding of serial murder are different from the ones described by scholars in the field, how do they differ?' 'My paper was a case analysis … I argue in my paper how their domineering mothers and their abusive childhoods caused them to become serial killers,' or its variations would often follow. I would then bang my head against the office wall in frustration after the student left.

There are several reasons why the conversations turned out that way. First, students did not know what a social science research paper was. Students who had written 10–12 pages of double-spaced text, it seemed, concluded that they had written a 'research paper.' That is, students had defined a research paper on length rather than its structure, form, and logic. Landrum (2008) refers to such papers as 'term papers' – papers that provide summaries of others' research findings. A 'research paper' on serial killers that simply rehashes existing works and theories of serial murder without a resolution of some sort is best described as a book report on steroids.

Second, students who want to write about serial killers base their understanding of the topic on what they have seen on television or in true-crime books rather than the scholarly research on serial murders. Had those students in my classes read two papers that David Canter (a British psychologist) and colleagues published in 2004, their understanding of serial murder would have been different. In Canter et al.'s (2004) article 'The organized/disorganized typology of serial murder: Myth or model?' published in *Psychology, Public Policy, and Law*, Canter et al. challenged the long-established typology that the agents at the Federal Bureau of Investigation (FBI) used as a way of classifying and profiling serial killers, and argued that the organized/disorganized typology inadequately differentiates the different types of serial killers. Then in that same year, Canter and Wentink (2004) published a paper in *Criminal Justice and Behavior* which tested Holmes and Holmes's (1994) typology of serial murder.

Ronald Holmes and colleagues had argued that serial killers could be differentiated from one another based on their motive (visionary, mission-oriented, hedonistic, or power-control-oriented). However, Canter and Wentink (2004) debunked that motive-based typology, showing that the classification of a single category based on motive was difficult due to overlapping features. Gabrielle Salfati (2000) also demonstrated that behaviors that occur in an offender's interactions with victims could be differentiated using the expressive/ instrumental distinction and frequency of crime scene behavior; in this set of findings, serial killers could be differentiated from ordinary killers based on the unusual and atypical ways in which they interacted with their victims (e.g., necrophilia). Had the students in my class on murder based their papers on the preceding journal publications rather than true-crime books, the beginning point of their papers would have been different. The research questions they asked would have been different.

Students make the preceding types of errors in their papers because they do not have an adequate understanding of the writing or the reading process. Writing a research paper is not like writing a novel: students do not 'develop' characters; they do not create conflicts between characters or within them. Instead, research papers resolve 'pre-existing conflicts between previous literature and current findings' (Landrum, 2008, p. 14). That is, by the time students begin to write, the literature has already been reviewed, the data have been analyzed, and they should already know how the paper will turn out; they should know if their results and/or arguments support or contradict the work others have done. All the preceding work should have been done in the prewriting process.

Yet, there are steps in the writing – prewriting – process that have been overlooked in previous research, and blindly presupposed in order for the preceding explanations to work. The first incorrect assumption is that writers cannot develop new ideas if they don't have new ideas. Research articles in social science journals are necessarily full of new ideas that have not been addressed in the current paper. There are always gaps or deficiencies in the literature (see Harris, 2014). That is why authors discuss limitations of their research and make recommendations for future works – as a tacit way of setting up the work they will do in the future or providing an itinerary for others who may want to do the work that was not done in the current paper. Writers are not able to develop new ideas because they have not learned to read critically.

The second flaw arises from a major omission in the accounting sequence. Let's say that an honors thesis student or a master's-level graduate student is writing a thesis on serial killers, and she has identified 50 peer-reviewed journal articles that have been published within the past 15 years – and she has read them. Then what? To be able to 'grimly describe each study' requires a tremendous amount of work and effort. To be able to even come up with a rough outline, the student will necessarily have had to process the literature in a particular way; and unless that student sat down with a blank sheet of paper and kept track of recurring themes, patterns, and deficiencies in the literature, the 'new idea' that should have emerged is apt to get lost in such unguided reading. Thus, previous works fail to address a logistic issue related to writing that actually precedes it – how to read in a way that promotes development and cultivation of new ideas prior to the outline – a Point of Critique (POC); and just as importantly, how to manage the information from the 'mass of past research.'

As undergraduate honors thesis students, as master's-level students, and then as doctoral-level students, most professors have all been there. I am sure they asked themselves, 'How do I organize, classify, and retrieve the relevant information for my own purpose?' during the writing process. Your instructors may have been lucky enough to stumble through that process by trial and error, even without a cogent theory of the practice behind it. About six years into my teaching career, I realized that students may not know that theory either. One reason that students may not know how to write social science research papers is that they have not been taught how to write them.

It is my contention that before students undertake any type of writing projects in a university, at the undergraduate and graduate level, they should first learn how to read. In the context of disciplines in social sciences, education, health sciences, and humanities, it is important for students to learn how to read journal articles, as most of the cutting-edge research and the debates within those disciplines will unfold in the pages of reputable peer-reviewed journal articles. Students will be expected to search, read, and assess journal articles more than any other types of text throughout their tenure as students. Furthermore, students should understand that the papers they write are guided by the direction of the literature on the topic that they have selected; they do not 'just' write a paper, willy-nilly. Instead, the research questions that students ask, the papers that require an original claim and finding of some sort begin with the critical reading that identifies shortcomings in the literature in some way. Students have to find a shortcoming and develop a Critique of Previous Literature (CPL). Those critiques should lead to research questions and their many revisions and reformulations throughout the reading process.

Students who struggle with writing papers generally do so because they have not read sufficiently; they attempt to say something novel and insightful without having an adequate command of the topic they have selected. Simply put, they do not know the literature. Reading and writing are related acts; one shapes the other. Students struggle with writing because they have not read sufficiently, carefully, or critically. Just as I advocate a regimented approach to reading, the same Spartan philosophy should dictate one's approach to writing.

Writing is not easy; it is tough work. Its difficulty and arduousness is qualitatively different from cleaning toilets, dealing with unruly customers in a retail store, lifting heavy objects all day, or trying to mediate a domestic dispute between two toothless drunks in a trailer park for the third time in one evening. The type of fatigue and stress that writing produces paralyzes the soul and damages one's self-esteem. When my own writing was not going well, there were days when I seriously thought about giving up academic life and trying something else. (I don't know what. As a short, stocky, bald, dim-witted Korean man with glasses, I really can't do much.) Then I recalled my experience in college working as a clerk where I had to clean toilets: the stench, the shame, and its pure wretchedness convinced me without a doubt that I did not want to clean toilets again – ever. I went back to writing in a day or two, after the sting of the painful rejection from a journal subsided. That is why the advice that general how-to books provide to treat writing like work is sound: we have to set schedules, 'clock in,' and do what the Nike commercials tell us we ought to do – just do it. By doing so, we dignify our activity as work and reproduce the moral order of writing as work.

Imagine a bus driver, a nurse, or a patrol officer who says things like, 'I must be inspired to [drive, take care of patients, answer 911 calls]' or 'I don't have the time to [drive, take care of patients, answer 911 calls].' People who harbored such thoughts and translated those hidden values into everyday behavior (as academics regularly do) would be out of a job yesterday. Only privileged academics can get away with talking such bovine scatology. The job of a faculty member at a university is to teach and write. If academics treat reading and writing in the same way ordinary people treat their work, then the idea of a psychological barrier to writing ought to be seen for what it is. Students need to treat writing papers as bus drivers treat driving, nurses treat attending to patients, and police officers treat answering 911 calls. It is your primary job in a university. It is not secondary to the numerous other jobs you may already have as a way of paying your bills.

As others have noted, writing is more than just typing. It entails prewriting activities such as 'reading, outlining, idea generation, and data analysis necessary for generating text' (Silvia, 2007, p. 18). Even prior to outlining, reading and note-taking may be just as implicative, if not more, than the actual writing, for it is during the act of reading that we decide what we might use in a paper (Landrum, 2008); it is during reading that we identify 'main themes, strengths, and weaknesses' in the literature (Cone & Foster, 2006, p. 103). In fact, Cone and Foster (2006) instruct their readers to keep a record of observations while reading in order to arrive at a major insight about a topic based on those observations. As can be seen, careful reading ought not to be treated as a secondary activity to writing; that proper reading may lead to insightful observations about a topic is already implied in the previous works. Students just have to learn how to read the literature in a way that cultivates insightful observations.

Framing blocks to writing as a problem of poor motivation is one way to diagnose the problem.

Writers who complain about:

> writer's block are writers who don't outline … After trying to write blindly, they feel frustrated and complain about how hard it is to generate words. No surprise – you can't write an article if you don't know what to write … get your thoughts in order before you try to communicate them to the world of science. (Silvia, 2007, p. 79)

That writing problems still get framed as problems of motivation is a bit puzzling, for academics do not write blindly – without any idea about how the paper will begin and end. By the time we have reviewed the literature, justified the reason for our study, collected the data or synthesized the literature for a review article, and conducted the study and analyzed the results, we ought to know, unequivocally, what we want to say in our papers. The same lesson applies to students who are writing their papers. By the time they begin the writing process, they ought to know exactly what they want to say in their papers. By the time all of the prewriting activities have been completed, the papers should almost write themselves.

Academics – and upper-level undergraduate students and first-year graduate students – do not know what to write or have trouble organizing their thoughts into papers because: (1) they have not read the literature sufficiently; or (2) they have read the literature sufficiently but have not found a way to organize the information gathered from their readings. Before one can put together an outline, one has to be familiar with the contents that will form the outline. Both of these errors lead to the type of writing problems that others have described. Both types of error occur at the reading level and ought to be remedied there.

The reading code sheet (RCOS) that I have developed systematizes the reading, note-taking, and organizing of voluminous amounts of information in an easily identifiable and retrievable format. This book explains how to use ten reading codes directly related to 'critical' reading of social science journal articles that others have presupposed but have not explored (e.g., SPL, CPL, GAP, RAT, RCL), and four codes necessary to critique and cultivate a reader's new ideas and claims (e.g., POC, MOP, WIL). By illuminating and elaborating on the previously assumed aspects of 'critical' reading, this book attempts to teach students how to read so that the major conceptual divisions and subdivisions of research papers and theses can be logically organized during the act of reading.

This book presents an alternative way to diagnose – hence resolve – a writer's block, and frames it as one of poor reading technique, execution, and management rather than motivation. Without adequate knowledge of the work of previous researchers, it is impossible to organize our own thoughts without appearing solipsistic or narcissistic. Without the right reading tools and techniques, we fall into the trap of simple summaries rather than logical critiques and anticipatable rationales – the big 'So what?' – for our papers. If students want to become competent scholars, there is only one way to achieve it: read, read, and then read some more.

2

Trying to Fix Mechanical and Structural Writing Problems with Abstract Tools

As undergraduate and graduate students, we have all experienced the magic acts that our teachers practiced on us. That is, we hand in a paper at the end of the semester, and when we receive our papers back, there is an inexplicable grade that appears at the top of the first page or at the bottom of the last page. Sometimes, there are a few laudatory phrases peppered here and there, but no systematic accounting of how the professor arrived at the grade. I do not ever recall any of the professors correcting mechanical or stylistic errors in the papers I had submitted, except one; I am quite certain I must have had countless structural, logical, and mechanical errors in the papers I turned in. My best guess now is that they were probably overwhelmed by the sheer number of mistakes and just gave up trying to correct them. After all, I was a product of the Chicago public school system at its nadir, and it probably showed in my work.

This 'magic' still persists – from what my own students tell me. They tell me that they continue to receive papers from their teachers that are marked with a letter or a numerical grade, without an adequate explanation of why they received the grade they did, how their teachers arrived at the grade, and what the students could do to improve their future performance. There is some truth to this complaint from students. However, I have also encountered students who have returned to school after they have graduated in order to pick up their papers; some of them even asked what they did wrong, and what they could do to improve their writing. In those moments, I would go over their papers and explain their errors and how to avoid making them in the future. While most were happy to just earn a passing grade, graduate, and move on with their lives, I have encountered some students who really wanted to improve their writing.

Being on the other end of the lectern, I can now understand why my teachers were reluctant to correct each and every grammatical mistake or fix an awkward sentence. Students should understand that fixing each and every grammatical error and awkward sentence is a time-consuming task, and almost impossible to accomplish on every single paper. That is, your teachers may begin a grading session with magnanimous and noble intentions, but such ideals fade away about an hour into the session. Furthermore, the students' papers that your teachers have to read, well, to be honest, are not all great. The good papers are easy to read and grade, for little disruption occurs during the reading process; the paragraphs are cogently organized; the sentences flow and tend to be well crafted. Badly written papers, on the other hand, elongate the reading and grading process: reading has to be interrupted every other sentence to mark and correct the error that has been made; sentences have to be read multiple times because they are awkward, ungrammatical, and do not flow; sometimes, the sentences do not even make sense; and your teachers have to struggle over how to politely bring that unpleasant news to your attention. Sometimes, your teachers find paragraphs that are so compressed together that it is not uncommon to find two to three ideas that have been 'mashed' into a large chunk of text that literally looks like a rectangle turned on its side.

Students should understand this fact: the sentences that you compose contain a history of all the successes and failures of your primary/elementary and high school education system. They also contain evidence of your personality, your study habits, the amount of time you spent writing the paper, and how much care and effort you put into it. If you spent all last night writing your paper, you may not think the consequences are evident because printed words on a page look the same, but as a reader, let me tell you unequivocally: your teachers know that you rushed through your paper and slapped it together at the last minute as you were slamming your third can of a caffeinated drink. If you spent at least a couple of weeks or more writing your paper so that the paragraphs are logically connected, fretting over which transition phrases to use for the umpteenth time, agonizing over the use of a period versus a semicolon, I want you to know that your instructors can literally see and feel the care and effort that you put into your work. Your soul is reflected in the sentences that you craft.

Sentences that students write are similar to clues that homicide offenders leave at their crime scenes. For example, a murderer who brings his own weapon (e.g., handgun, knife) to the scene of the crime suggests a particular type of an offender, with a very specific objective in mind; this type of offender is different from someone who uses weapons that are already at the scene (e.g., lamp, beer stein) to kill a victim. Both types of offender are qualitatively and quantitatively different. The behaviors that both types of offender engage in have been shown to vary, empirically. The same could be said of students' writing. First, there are the structural errors that differentiate one paper and one student from another; then there are the mechanical, stylistic, and grammatical errors that further differentiate one paper and student from another. As an example, students who use semicolons to connect dependent and subordinate clauses to the main clause make that error primarily because they do not know the proper rule regarding semicolon use. Students whose papers are littered with fragments are a bit more disconcerting. The repeated occurrence of fragments in students' papers suggests they have a fundamental problem with the basic rules of English composition. Unless that basic problem is fixed, it will be pointless to work on other rules of grammar or composition. Thus, the sentences that you – the students – write are like evidence at a crime scene: your professor, instructor, teacher – whatever you call the person who stands behind a lectern at a four-year institution of higher learning – 'sees' the author behind your sentences. Imagine collecting, bagging, tagging, and processing all the pieces of evidence at a crime scene. That work would be laborious and painstaking. So it just may be the sheer volume of work involved that dissuades your teacher from making extended comments on your papers. Or there may be other reasons that are obvious to other instructors which I can't repeat here.

I was observing that students were making similar types of errors in their papers; and because I needed to be able to provide a justification of the assigned grade, and because I was tired of writing the same comments, I initially created a grading code sheet. I noticed that students – undergraduate and graduate – were making recurring errors in their papers. For instance, they would write sentences that sounded awkward, so the code AWK was created. Students would assert a claim, but without citing or substantiating the source, so the code CITE was formed. Students would try to 'BS' their way through some papers, so the code LMG (Largely Magnified Generalities) was created. Students would fail to use paragraphs so the code NP (need to use paragraphs/need a new paragraph) was developed; sometimes, students would write long-winded sentences that could be reduced to one succinct sentence so the code TLW (Too Long-winded) came into existence. Some assertions made in the paper were so incredible and outlandish that the code JOK (is this a joke?) was added. (In criminology, such I-can't-believe-s/he-said-that and are-you-kidding-me? paper comments are usually related to student sentences on race and crime.)

After trying out the codes and seeing modest success, I wondered if it would be possible to teach grammar through such a system. I found that students needed concrete and specific advice on how to construct better sentences, use correct punctuation marks, etc. So I began to collect information on students' grammatical errors. I discovered that most of the errors students make could be corrected if they consulted Strunk and White's (1979) *The Elements of Style*. The grading code sheet was expanded even more to include page and section references to Strunk and White (SSW: See Strunk and White).

Now, I could underline, circle, and highlight particular sentences, words, phrases and identify a problem to a student; I could also show students what needed to be fixed in their papers, and suggest concrete changes that needed to be made. Moreover, I could impose penalty points each and every time an error occurred to demonstrate how I arrived at the numerical grade that appeared on a student's paper. The value of the penalty points was entirely arbitrary and subjective. Thus, if a student made 15 errors in a 10-page paper, and if each penalty was a 3-point deduction, the student could be penalized for a total of 45 points out of a possible total point value of 100. I began to notice that students' writings were improving little by little. Once students realized where they needed to fix the problems and how to go about fixing them, they did so. A penalty for each and every error was probably a highly motivating factor. I recently asked and students confirmed that they wanted to avoid repeated penalties.

There were three principal reasons why I developed the grading code sheet. One, I wanted to minimize grade appeals from students. Grade appeals just took a lot of work due to the number of forms that had to be filled out. I had enough paperwork to do. I needed to be able to justify the grade I gave out. Second, I just got tired of saying the same things on students' papers. They would make the same mistakes over and over again, and my hand would literally ache from writing the same comments on students' papers. I wanted to minimize such repetition. Third, and most importantly, I was a teacher. That role and identity meant – still means – a lot to me. If I didn't fix those writing problems, then who would? I could have defined out of the problem rather easily (Muir, 1977): I could have justified easy or minimal grading by stating my need to produce articles for tenure. I could have blamed the English teachers in college, high school, and primary school who had failed to properly teach students the mechanics of writing. I could have blamed the moon and its pull on the ocean if I wanted to define out of my role as a teacher. But that would have been inconsistent with what my own teacher(s) had done, and it would have violated the code of professionalism.

For example, imagine a uniformed patrol officer who receives a radio dispatch about a citizen who needs assistance because intruders are breaking down her door. The officer thinks the call might be dangerous, so s/he decides to ignore the call. In my work with patrol officers, I found that whatever biases they harbored, whatever personal attitudes they held, they never let those personal beliefs interfere with the performance of their professional duties. I would often ask patrol officers why they did certain things, and the answer was almost always, 'I'm the police. It's my job.' That is the only justification they needed to perform their duties. Now, I am not trying to excuse cases where such self-justified ideologies go awry. This book is not the place to argue about the causes and consequences of police misconduct. I am simply making the point that police officers I met and interacted with never let other conflicting ideologies or ambiguities confound their roles as professionals. Once I came to view my own work as a teacher along such lines, I found it difficult to define out of my professional duties and obligations. Teachers who see problems with students' writing and do not attempt to fix them are like uniformed patrol officers who receive a call on their radio from a distressed citizen and do nothing. Both have no business being in their line of work.

There are two grading codes (EXQ: Excessive Quotes; and POC: Point of Critique) that I want to elaborate on. These codes were developed because I saw similar recurring errors in undergraduate and graduate student literature reviews, research papers, and theses. For example, I noticed that upper-level undergraduates and graduate students were excessively quoting (defined as more than two full lines in a submitted paper) an author if the author's main points were particularly abstruse or difficult to paraphrase; excessive quotes appeared in papers because students had not understood the author adequately – or the students were just being lazy. In essence, students were able to let the quoted author do the work of explaining a concept rather than doing the work themselves: the use of excessive quotes resulted in the development of the code EXQ. I also noticed that students would merely move from the concatenation of summaries of previous works to the data and methods section without adequately providing a critique of the literature or developing their own point of critique (POC), thereby providing an insufficient rationale of why the student's own paper was warranted. I then realized that upper-level undergraduate students and graduate students needed a different type of guidance to complete their papers – more than what the grading code sheet could provide. Consequently, I began to mine their papers for patterns in their errors. Before I could remedy the problems, I first needed to figure out what the problems were.

One type of error immediately stood out, and I am sure most instructors in undergraduate and graduate classes have seen this type of error in the literature reviews, research papers, and first drafts of theses that students submit. The error involves citing one author repeatedly in one paragraph as part of a literature review. In the course of one to three or more paragraphs, rather than summarizing the work of previous researchers in some principled and methodical way, in a way that is logically and thematically connected, the student will make several points using one author, in the process citing the said author ad nauseam. Then the student will move on to make several other summaries using another author, citing the new author ad nauseam. I will refer to this practice as 'beating one horse to death.'

31

What was missing from the typical papers I received from fourth-year undergraduate students and first-year graduate students were critiques of the literature. Students were already good at summarizing previous works. After all, simple summaries – term papers – are just book reports on growth hormones. However, they had trouble figuring out how to critique what they were reading. I mistakenly believed that such problems could be remedied by working on their writing: I tried to develop codes to help students improve their writing, but to no avail. Then I began to think that one way of improving the structural organization of student papers was to critically re-examine the reading process.

3

Should I Even Read This?

How to Read the Abstract, General Introduction, and Methods Sections

Let's assume that you – the student – have searched a database of some sort (e.g., Psychinfo, Social Science Citation Index) to check the number of articles that have been published within the past 20 years on the topic you have selected for a research paper, and the results appear to be unwieldy. For the sake of illustration, let's assume that you get 200 'hits' from the topic words you searched. That is too many to manage, let alone read, so you narrow the search terms and now the results page indicates 70 hits. That is much more manageable. So you peruse the titles; some of the recent works definitely appear to be related to the topic you want to write about – the title is unmistakable. We will say that 40 articles will be included in your literature review because the titles are relevant or because you are sufficiently familiar with the research area to know that certain scholars who have appeared on the list are always cited in relation to the topic you searched and need to be included. Ten articles appear to be irrelevant to your topic, so they are excluded. You are not sure about the remaining 20 articles. From the titles of the papers, they appear to be related to your topic, but you are not sure. What to do at this point? One, you could just go with the 40 articles that you found and ignore the remaining 20, and risk missing out on some important and relevant points – points that might have altered how you might frame your research. Or, you can read the abstract, and then determine if the article is worth including in your literature review or not. Others have called this practice 'skimming' or 'scanning'; however, those terms do not do justice to how the abstract should really be read.

An abstract is a very, very brief summary of a journal article. Most journal publications require an abstract of some sort, which range from 100 to 200 words. Reading through an abstract is less time-consuming than reading the full-length article. An abstract contains enough essential information about the article to be able to assess its merit and relevance. In the less than two minutes it takes to read through an abstract, you can discern and anticipate the logic of the author's argument before even reading through the full article. Even in medical and hard science journals, the format of a research article is similar to that of a social science article: background, materials and methods, results, discussion, and conclusion. In an abstract, those five components are covered in one way or another. And whether the student is reading the article as part of the literature review or trying to decide if the article is pertinent enough to the chosen topic to be included, reading should begin with the abstract. While reading the abstract, the reading codes ought to be written where relevant in the right margin of the hard copy of the article. There is a reason why the codes should be written in the right margin. After the reading is completed, thematic codes will be written in the left margin as a way of classifying and organizing recurring patterns and themes in the literature. The right margin is reserved for the reading codes while the left is reserved for thematic codes.

How to Read the Abstract

In the section below, the abstracts of four published articles from reputable journals have been reproduced. To describe the function of the words in the abstract, and for accessibility, clarity, and ease of reference, each sentence has been numbered consecutively.

The abstract in DiCataldo and Everett's (2008) article on 'Distinguishing juvenile homicide from violent juvenile offending,' published in *International Journal of Offender Therapy and Comparative Criminology*, is exactly 151 words. The abstract is composed of seven sentences. Now, consider the type of information that is contained in the abstract:

(1) Juvenile homicide is a social problem that has remained a central focus within juvenile justice research in recent years. (2) The term juvenile murderer describes a legal category, but it is purported to have significant scientific meaning. (3) Research has attempted to conceptualize adolescent murderers as a clinical category that can be reliably distinguished from their nonhomicidal counterparts. (4) This study examined 33 adolescents adjudicated delinquent or awaiting trial for murder and 38 adolescents who committed violent, nonhomicidal offenses to determine whether the two groups differed significantly on family history, early development, delinquency history, mental health, and weapon possession variables. (5) The nonhomicide

group proved more problematic on many of these measures. (6) Two key factors did distinguish the homicide group: These adolescents endorsed the greater availability of guns and substance abuse at the time of their commitment offenses. (7) The significance of this finding is discussed, and the implications for risk management and policy are reviewed.

Sentences #1–3 do the type of work that could be described as Summary of Previous Literature (SPL). This type of a sentence provides a general background on the topic you have selected, and summarizes the results from previous studies. In this abstract, the previous literature has been framed along the theme of (#1) time, (#2) definitions, (#3) distinguishing characteristics. Sentences #2 and #3 tacitly hint at a Critique of Previous Literature (CPL), but those missing gaps (GAPS) are not explicitly stated. In a CPL, the author you are reading is providing a critique and pointing out a limitation of the previous and existing works; GAP highlights missing elements, deficiencies, and limitations in the current state of knowledge in some systematic way.

Sentences like #4 in the abstract convey what the authors of the paper are doing. Those types of sentences in general are best represented by the reading code WTD: What They (the authors) Do. This code captures the main research question that the authors pose and resolve in their text. In abstracts, WTDs not only describe the main problems the papers address but they also describe the materials and methods used for the study. Simply put, WTDs are what the article is about. WTD sentences usually begin with phrases like, 'This paper examines ...' 'In this paper ...' 'This paper attempts to ...' WTDs generally appear in three places in most social science journal articles: abstract, introduction, and conclusion (WTDD: What They Did).

There is a reason that the code WTD is used rather than the more accepted 'thesis' or 'thesis statement.' Some use thesis statement to indicate a conclusion of sorts – 'a case developed using existing knowledge, sound evidence, and reasoned argument' (Machi & McEvoy, 2012, p. 1). If the thesis statement refers to a conclusion of sorts, then what is an appropriate way to describe the conclusion section that always appears at the end of journal articles? Some use the term 'argument' or 'main idea' to refer to a similar point (Lipson, 2005; Osmond, 2013). Finally, the term thesis is used to indicate the final product that undergraduate and graduate students produce as part of their requirements to fulfill their degrees (i.e., BA, MA, and PhD). The words 'thesis' and 'thesis statement' have too many meanings: they are likely to lead to confusion. Hence, I have avoided the terms.

Sentences #5 and #6 present the Results of Findings (ROF). ROFs describe the primary results – main claims – of the journal article that you are reading. This code is usually found in three places in a social science journal article: abstract, results section, and the discussion/conclusion. There are two main

ROFs that are noteworthy in the preceding article. The ROFs should tell you if the article you are reading is relevant to your own research topic or not. In scanning an article and reading through an abstract, the ROF should be the nugget that ought to be mined for, as this will tell you if the article is related to your own paper and topic. If the ROF suggests that the article you are reading is not pertinent to your topic and the paper you are writing, then that article probably should not be included in your literature review, and you should not read on any further. Sentence #7 discusses the implications of the findings. Readers are not told what the implications are, just that implications exist. Those implications are not revealed because the authors are constrained by the space and word limits imposed on abstracts.

In reading through one 151-word abstract, we have at least a general idea of what the paper is about. The readers are introduced to the background (SPL), possible critiques (CPL/GAP), what the authors are doing in their work

FIGURE 2

as a way of improving the gap in the literature (WTD), and the results of their findings (ROF). These reading codes ought to be marked in the right margin of the text, next to the sentences that exemplify that code (Figure 2). Therefore, sentences #1–3 should be bracketed and the code SPL written in the right margin. Next to sentence #4 the code WTD ought to be inserted; next to sentences #5 and #6 the code ROF ought to be inserted.

The abstract in Hattie and Timperley's (2007) article 'The power of feedback,' published in *Review of Educational Research*, is exactly 145 words. The abstract is composed of six sentences. Again, consider the type of information that is contained in the abstract:

(1) Feedback is one of the most powerful influences on learning and achievement, but this impact can be either positive or negative. (2) Its power is frequently mentioned in articles about teaching, but surprisingly few recent studies have systematically investigated its meaning. (3) This article provides a conceptual analysis of feedback and reviews the evidence related to its impact on learning and achievement. (4) This evidence shows that although feedback is among the major influences, the type of feedback and the way it is given can be differentially effective. (5) A model of feedback is then proposed that identifies the particular properties and circumstances that make it effective, and some typically thorny issues are discussed, including the timing of feedback and the effects of positive and negative feedback. (6) Finally, this analysis is used to suggest ways in which feedback can be used to enhance its effectiveness in classrooms.

Sentence #1 describes what could be called an SPL, for the authors are simply providing background information on the previous literature. In the first sentence, the authors summarize the literature on feedback into one concise sentence, telling readers that feedback can work in positive and negative ways. Sentence #1 should be bracketed and the code SPL should be written in the right margin. In the very next sentence, the authors mention that the power of feedback is often noted in articles related to teaching, again signaling that the clause is performing the work of an SPL, but the disjunction marker 'but' hints that something else may be emerging.

What appears in the second clause is the following assertion: 'surprisingly few recent studies have systematically investigated its meaning.' Clauses like that do not summarize the previous literature. The second clause points to what has not been done in the literature on feedback. Clauses and sentences like that point to a negation – what is not being done – and illustrate a Critique of Previous Literature (CPL) that the authors are pointing out. Logically, that critique leads to a shortcoming or a GAP in the literature. The code CPL/GAP should be written in the right margin. Within the first two sentences, the authors have summarized the literature on feedback and identified a shortcoming within that literature.

What happens after a GAP is pointed out? Sentence #3 introduces the reader to what the paper is about or what the authors will do in their paper (WTD). Again, phrases like, 'This paper examines ...' 'In this article ...' 'This article provides ...' tell the readers the main research question that is being asked in the text. If we were to frame this WTD into a standard research question, it might look like the following: 'How does feedback impact student learning and achievement?' The question is elegantly simple, but profoundly meaningful, for in their article, Hattie and Timperley (2007) will review existing works and provide a conceptual analysis of how feedback affects students. According to the authors, such a question has not been asked in previous literature.

And in sentence #4 the authors provide the Results of their Findings (ROF), that type of feedback and the way it is delivered have different effects; in sentence #5, the authors propose a conceptual model of effective feedback. Both sentences describe an ROF; those sentences should be highlighted and the code ROF should be written in the right margin. The ROF should be highlighted because it is the most significant piece of information from that article. This main finding – claim – should determine if this article should be included in a student's review of the literature or not.

The abstract in Pritchard and Hughes's (1997) article on 'Patterns of deviance in crime news,' published in the *Journal of Communication*, is exactly 133 words. Consider the work that the sentences in the abstract perform:

(1) Existing research has failed to develop a satisfactory theoretical explanation for journalists' decisions about which crimes to highlight and which to ignore. (2) We proposed that four forms of deviance (normative deviance, statistical deviance, status deviance, and cultural deviance) account for much of the variation in decisions about crime news. (3) To test deviance-based explanations for crime news, we conducted a comprehensive investigation of Milwaukee, WI, homicides and how two newspapers covered them. (4) We used content analysis and interviews with journalists. (5) The results showed that the newsworthiness of a homicide is enhanced when Whites are suspects or victims, males are suspects, and victims are females, children, or senior citizens. (6) We concluded that status deviance and cultural deviance are important components of newsworthiness and that statistical deviance (unusualness) may be much less important than commonly assumed.

The presence of the word 'failed' after 'existing research' should be a clue that sentence #1 is pointing out a CPL/GAP of some sort; in the sentences that follow, that is what the readers are told. Sentence #1 is an example of

CPL/GAP. What is the missing element in the existing literature? A 'satisfactory theoretical explanation' that explains why journalists highlight some crimes while ignoring others. Sentences #2–4 describe the WTD, for they describe the materials and methods as well the main research questions being addressed in their study. Sentences #5–6 describe the ROF. The SPL is implicitly contained in the words 'commonly assumed,' but readers are not explicitly told what it is. The codes, CPL/GAP, WTD, and ROF ought to be written in the right margin of the article next to the respective sentences. Again, even without adequate background knowledge of the literature or SPL, the ROFs ought to tell you – the reader – if the main claims made in the article are pertinent for your ends. Readers know that status deviance and cultural deviance constitute 'important components of newsworthiness.'

The abstract in Kim, Hogge, Ji, Shim, and Lothspeich's (2014) article, 'Hwa-Byung among middle-aged Korean women: Family relationships, gender-role attitudes, and self-esteem,' published in *Health Care for Women International*, is exactly 100 words. Notice how their abstract is organized:

(1) We surveyed 395 Korean middle-aged women and examined how their perceptions of family relationships, gender-role attitudes, and self-esteem were associated with Hwa-Byung (HB; Korean Anger Syndrome). (2) Our regression analyses revealed that participants who reported worse family relationship problems experienced more HB symptoms. (3) Having profeminist, egalitarian attitudes toward women's gender roles was also associated with more HB symptoms. (4) Self-esteem was not significantly associated with HB. (5) Based on the results, we suggest that what is crucial to understanding HB is not how women evaluate themselves, but rather the level of stress caused by family relationship problems and their perception of women's roles.

Sentence #1 does not summarize or critique the previous literature; rather, it tells the reader what the article is about. Therefore, the most appropriate code to write in the right margin is WTD. Again, notice how the research question is embedded in the WTD. If we were to turn this assertion into a research question, it would resemble the following: 'How are middle-aged Korean women's perceptions of their family relationships, gender-role attitudes, and self-esteem associated with Hwa-Byung?' In sentences #2 and #3, the authors provide the results of their study (ROF). These two sentences should be highlighted, for they constitute the important pieces of information to be gleaned from this article. After reading the abstract, readers ought to be able to tell if the full paper is relevant to their own projects. If a student is writing a paper about mental illness and women's mental health, this article should be included in her literature review.

As one can observe, there is some variance in the way the abstracts are composed. Some abstracts provide SPL and CPL while others do not; some abstracts use two sentences to describe their ROFs while others expend one to do the work. And when students are not sure whether or not an article should be included in their literature review – and the title of the paper does not provide adequate clues about the paper's pertinence to their chosen topic – the abstract should be read to discern if the primary findings (ROF) of the studies being read are consistent with the proposed topic and aim of the student's paper. Furthermore, even after an article has been deemed to be relevant for inclusion in one's literature review, the abstract should be read first so that the logic of the author's argument embedded in the article can be rehearsed and anticipated in the subsequent sections.

As stated earlier, certain components of an article will appear more than once throughout the article. For example, ROFs are found in the abstract, the results, and the discussion and conclusion. Similarly, the rationale (RAT) for why a particular study is necessary and warranted cannot appear randomly and out of the blue. It has to follow a logical, linear, and anticipatable path of reasoning and argumentation (Jordan & Zanna, 1999). This logical 'set-up' unfurls in the literature review section; its shadow is implicitly cast in the abstract.

The use of reading codes can also serve as a guide to students for how to construct an abstract. One sentence can describe the SPL, another the CPL. The SPL and the CPL ought to at least tacitly suggest a GAP, which logically leads to the WTD. One to two sentences can be used to describe the WTD, including the materials and methods. One to two sentences could be used to describe the ROF, with a final sentence for implications of results. With a minimum of five sentences, then, a student ought to be able to craft an abstract of her own, without wondering about its constitutive elements.

By noting the primary function of words, sentences, and paragraphs in texts, readers are able to structure their reading so that the contents of what they have read can be organized and classified along predictable, anticipatable, and recurring patterns. In this section, I have shown students how to read abstracts. In subsequent sections and chapters, I will show how to read much longer blocks of text using the reading codes. Thus, rather than reading social science articles without boundaries (unstructured reading), the reading codes provide textual, cognitive, and conceptual boundaries so that readers do not engage in mindless and meandering reading. By actively engaging with the text (and the author), readers of social science articles should not ask, 'What did I just read for the past 30 minutes?' Those types of questions arise because texts are too difficult to decipher (e.g., Jacques Lacan, Immanuel Kant, Judith Butler) or the mind has wandered away during the act of reading because of an absence of structure to the reading.

By identifying the function of texts and writing the codes in the right margin, readers achieve three objectives.

1. Slowing down the act of reading. The use of reading codes structures the mind toward a purposive task, thereby delineating cognitive boundaries.
2. Organizing the contents of the reading into recurring themes (e.g., SPL, CPL, GAP, ROF) that can be easily retrieved for writing purposes.
3. Identifying potential GAPs so that the reader could anticipate the RAT (see Chapter 5) from the given CPL and GAP for use in their own papers.

How to Read the General Introduction

An introduction, as the word denotes, appears at the beginning of something; it does not appear at the end, for that would make it a conclusion. An introduction in a social science journal article is like a blueprint and a map: it lays out the itinerary of an article's path of logical travel. Introductions are longer than abstracts but shorter than literature review sections. Introductions tend to be between two and four paragraphs; they are also organized and structured into predictable patterns. Consider the following introduction from Gruenewald, Pizarro, and Chermak's (2009) article on 'Race, gender, and the newsworthiness of homicide incidents,' published in *Journal of Criminal Justice.*

There are four paragraphs that make up the introduction. In the first paragraph, second sentence, the authors write, 'Scholars have found that crime is generally a staple of news programming, comprising from 10 to 50 percent of all news stories [citations omitted]' (p. 262). Sentences like this summarize the state of the literature, so the code SPL ought to be written in the available margin. The first five sentences are written in a similar spirit, as a way of summarizing previous literature. Then in the last sentence of the first paragraph, the authors write, 'Despite such increased attention, an empirical void remains in the literature regarding the factors that contribute to the decision-making process ...' (p. 262). Sentences like this critique the previous literature (CPL) and identify a GAP in the knowledge base. In one paragraph, the authors have summarized the literature and provided a critique of, and identified a gap in, the existing literature.

The first sentence of the second paragraph reads, 'To date, few studies [citations omitted] have seriously considered how the gender and race of homicide victims and offenders, and their interaction, affect news media selection and prominence decisions, and whether these interactions supersede incident characteristics in increasing the newsworthiness of a particular homicide' (p. 262). Again, the sentence points to a CPL and identifies a GAP in it: few studies have examined how gender and race affect the decision-making process in the news.

The rest of the sentences in the paragraph go on to provide other shortcomings in the literature (e.g., criteria used to assess newsworthiness; lack of Hispanics in previous study samples; lack of a specific examination of race and gender). Thus far, in the first paragraph, the authors have provided a broad summary of the literature, ending it with a critique. In the second paragraph, the authors have put forth more GAPs that exist in the literature. So what? Why should these GAPs matter?

   The authors answer that, 'The scholarly understanding of newsworthiness criteria is important for several reasons' (Gruenewald et al., 2009, p. 262). They list three. The answers to the 'So what?' question constitute a rationale for the study (RAT): our proposed work is warranted and necessary because others have not addressed the GAPs. Every study and/or experiment has to be able to answer this question. After the three RATs are proffered, the WTD appears in the fourth paragraph: 'This study examined the relationship between homicide participant and incident characteristics and news media decision-making in the city of Newark, New Jersey' (p. 262). Again, WTD tells readers what will be done in the paper. In the rest of the article, the authors will remedy the GAPs they have identified. The general introduction, very much similar to an abstract, provides a taste of the full-course meal to emerge in the rest of the article. In the preceding introduction, that initial 'taste' is offered in the form of SPL→CPL→GAP→ RAT→WTD in four paragraphs.

   Notice how this pattern is mirrored again in Gershenfeld's (2014) article 'A review of undergraduate mentoring programs,' published in *Review of Educational Research*. Similar to the Gruenewald et al.'s (2009) article, Gershenfeld's (2014) introduction is composed of four paragraphs. In the first two sentences of the first paragraph, Gershenfeld (2014, p. 365) writes,

> Research on mentoring has not kept pace with the proliferation of under-graduate mentoring programs (UMPs) on college campuses [citations omitted]. The purpose of establishing UMPs can vary, but they generally aim to strengthen student engagement and relationship building in order to improve academic performance and college retention, and/or assist with career planning [citation omitted].

The negation marker in the first sentence suggests that the sentence could be a CPL, but it could also function as an SPL. In such cases, it is best to move on and examine the next sentence; the second sentence definitely functions as an SPL so that code should be written in the right margin. The third sentence is a bit more explicit: 'However, without methodologically rigorous and valid research, it is unknown if mentoring programs are achieving their intended outcomes' (p. 365). The author is now critiquing the state of research on under-graduate mentoring programs; she is claiming that previous research has not assessed the merits of mentoring programs in methodologically valid ways.

Sentences like that illustrate a CPL, which logically points to a shortcoming in the literature (GAP).

What does Gershenfeld do after she has identified a GAP in the literature? Consider sentence #4: 'With universities heavily investing both financial and human resources in mentoring, it is prudent that research guide the development and continuous improvements in mentoring programs for undergraduate students' (p. 365). If we now ask the brutally simple 'So what?' question of Gershenfeld, how would she answer it? If readers asked of her why her topic, her paper, and her GAP are significant, how would she answer that question? Sentence #4 provides an answer to the 'So what?' question. Sentences like #4 would illustrate a RAT. Once this RAT is provided, notice the next sentence that follows: 'This article is the third review of studies that examine the impact of UMPs' (p. 365) – in other words a WTD.

Notice the recurring pattern here: in one paragraph, Susan Gershenfeld has broadly summarized the literature on undergraduate mentoring programs (SPL); critiqued the research by pointing out that it is unknown whether such programs are accomplishing what they purport to accomplish (CPL); stated why that shortcoming in the literature is important (RAT); and how she will remedy that shortcoming in the literature (WTD). The WTD logically appears after the SPL, CPL, and RAT. As a 'taste' of the full argument to emerge in the rest of the sections of her paper, the first paragraph takes readers from a broadly formulated SPL to a WTD in one sublime paragraph. Most introductions are not that structurally elegant.

In the next two paragraphs, the author SPLs prior research, summarizing and critiquing the previous literature in greater detail. Then in the fourth and final paragraph, Gershenfeld writes the following sentence: 'The value of this current review is fivefold' (p. 366). She then goes on to flesh out what those values are: (1) her paper extends the review of UMPs from 2008 to 2012, thus covering the period omitted in a previous researcher's period of study. (2) She assesses the methodological rigor of previous studies using evidence-based criteria. (3) She evaluates the role of the mentor in previous studies. (4) She incorporates social validity as a measure. (5) Finally, she identifies key features of mentoring programs from previous studies. In other words, Gershenfeld provides five separate and distinct answers to the 'So what?' question or five RATs for why her paper is necessary and warranted. Readers do not have to wonder why her paper and topic are important. She provides readers with five good reasons.

Shumaker and Prinz's (2000) review article 'Children who murder: A review,' published in *Clinical Child and Family Psychology Review*, has four paragraphs that make up the introduction. The first sentence of the first paragraph begins with, 'Though homicidal youth have received considerable attention in the media and in the social sciences, children under age 13 who committed homicide are understudied' (p. 97). That is, the authors provide a summary of the literature ('homicidal youth have received considerable attention in the media and in the social sciences'), and a critique of the previous literature (but 'children under age 13 who committed homicide are understudied'). Thus far, the sequence of the logic of ideas in the first paragraph of the introduction can be represented by the reading codes SPL→CPL→GAP.

If a GAP exists in the literature, so what? Why should that deficiency matter? Why should anyone care? Consider Shumaker and Prinz's (2000) answer to the 'So what?' question: 'Despite the low base rate, preteen offenders should be studied for several reasons' (p. 97). They list three reasons why the topic is important and should be studied: (1) young killers pose problems for the juvenile justice system; (2) juvenile homicide rates have doubled; (3) for prevention purposes. These are the RATs for why their work is important. RAT, again, follows the GAP in the logical sequence of how ideas in introductions are structurally organized. Since Shumaker and Prinz (2000) are writing a review article in a psychology journal, the third paragraph elaborates on how the authors selected the published studies to be included in their review paper.

In the last paragraph of the introduction, the authors write, 'The review examines classification schemes and typologies of youthful homicide, predictors of homicidal behavior in children, and how childhood behavioral characteristics of adult murderers, particularly adult serial killers, might bear on the study of preteen homicide' (p. 98). The occurrence of the first three words of the paragraph 'The review examines' ought to signal that the sentence and/or paragraph will be related to what the paper is about – WTD. In four paragraphs, the authors have summarized the literature (SPL), critiqued it (CPL), and by doing so they have identified a shortcoming (GAP), which has served as a rationale (RAT) for why their paper is warranted – why someone should care. The last paragraph tells readers what the authors will do in the paper (WTD).

As can be seen, introductions, like abstracts, are not formless; they have a logical form and structure. As appetizers before the main course – the literature review, data and methods, and results – they provide an outline and a map of what is to come in the rest of the article. When students are reading social science journal articles, they should follow the logic and form that is already inherent in them. As shown here, abstracts are organized in a way that is predictable and anticipatable. The reading codes ought to be used as boundary markers so that students know what they are reading, page by page, paragraph by paragraph, line by line. Thus, the ideas contained in the abstract should appear in the introduction, and the ideas in the introduction elaborated to a greater extent in the literature review. And by using the reading codes, students should be able to anticipate the next item to appear in the article; if the reading codes are used during the act of reading, students should never have to ask 'Where is this article going?' or 'What's the author trying to do?' The answers to those questions should emerge naturally and ineluctably from the way social science journal articles are structured and organized.

When students become adept at reading, they will begin asking themselves, 'Will this assertion that is fraught with tension be resolved in the subsequent sections?' (WIL). Such questions arise because the reader has already anticipated several potential paths of the author's logic and her argument's possible itinerary. If the author fails to connect logically related points, the reader will note that she missed an obvious theoretical, conceptual, and analytical connection to earlier works (MOP). Sometimes, the reader may 'see' points that even the author did not intend or anticipate. Such omissions in the text that you are reading do not point out any limitations and gaps; rather, the stated point could be used as a Point of Critique (POC) in a future paper. That is, a Relevant Point to Pursue (RPP) and mine in another paper.

How to Read the Data and Methods Section

One of the primary objectives of the methods section parallels the hallmark of science – reproducibility. That is, those interested enough – for whatever reason – in a study ought to be able to recreate its conditions sufficiently so that the results could be challenged or confirmed. According to Jordan and Zanna (1999, p. 464), readers ought to pay attention to the following guidelines while reading methods sections: (1) how the independent and dependent variables are measured, and (2) do the measures accurately reflect the intended concepts? This means if a student wants to critique the previous literature (CPL) on methodological grounds, then the deficiency in the current article or literature is a limitation and a GAP that the student could exploit as a way of remedying the gap in the literature (POC).

Consider how Piquero, Farrington, Nagin, and Moffitt (2010, p. 157) measured 'life failure' of men at ages 32 and 48 based on history of employment, relationships, substance abuse, mental health, criminal justice involvement, and self-reported delinquency. If the men at those ages scored high they were considered failures in life; a low score indicated success in life. So what constitutes a high score? If the men kept an unclean apartment or home, or moved more than twice within the past five years, that would be counted as life failure. Furthermore, if the men were not living with a female partner, or had been divorced within the past five years, or did not 'get along well with female partner,' the men would have been counted as a life failure. If the men had self-reported offenses in the past five years (excluding theft from work and tax fraud) they would have been counted as life failures. There are six other measures of life success and failure. Although an established and accepted way of measuring psychopathy and antisocial personalities, I am sure that readers could find a way to critique those measures. An astute graduate student can find a way to argue that the purported measures do not accurately reflect the intended concepts. The grounds on which you – the student – could critique the measures used illustrates a Point of Critique (POC). Or one could find issue with the statistical tests that are used. If a previous study used a single measure, your POC could be that only one measure was used, and that you will remedy that GAP by using multiple measures.

   Jordan and Zanna (1999) provide detailed instructions on how to read quantitatively designed social psychology journal articles. However, social science journal articles are not exclusively composed of quantitative studies. There are qualitative – non-statistical – approaches to data and analysis. Reading qualitative social science journal articles, however, is somewhat similar to reading quantitatively designed studies. Consider Stephen Lyng's (1990) article entitled, 'Edgework: A social psychological analysis of voluntary risk taking' that was published in the *American Journal of Sociology*. In this article, Stephen Lyng introduces a new concept to explain various forms of voluntary risk-taking activities (e.g. sky-diving, motorcycle racing); he does so by drawing on a rich theoretical tradition in sociology (e.g., Marx, Mead). So how did the author arrive at the new concept? What data did he use?

> As a jump pilot, I was able to observe the most intimate details of the group's activities. These observations were recorded in the form of field notes written up at the end of most weekends at the drop zone (an area approved by the FAA for parachute drops) and after many sky-diver social events. The accuracy of participant-observational data was also checked in intensive semistructured interviews with strategic respondents. In these interviews, which totaled scores of hours, respondents were asked to describe the experience of dealing with the various risks associated with the sport. (Lyng, 1990, p. 856)

Lyng conducted semistructured interviews with sky-divers. Based on the respondents' answers, the author identified recurring patterns in the data that led to three analytical categories: (1) various types of edgework activities; (2) specific individual capacities relevant to edgework; (3) sensations associated with edgework. Note that no independent and dependent variables were measured. That is because in qualitative research, hypotheses are not tested as much as they are generated. In qualitative research – whether the form of the data is ethnographic text, transcriptions of interviews, or historical documents – the data are collated and classified into distinct analytical categories based on the principle of induction (Strauss, 1987). Those analytical categories 'emerge' from the textual data.

To develop a POC from the analytical categories, readers can question the validity of the theoretical concept the author introduces: does the measure accurately reflect the intended concepts? That is, are the activities that Lyng lists as edgework sufficiently reflective of the concept of edgework? Moreover, readers can critique the fact that insufficient details were presented in the paper. Thus, how many participants did the ethnographer interview? How were the participants selected? How long did these interviews last? Were the respondents paid? And so on. These are all valid potential POCs that could be used to remedy methodological GAPs in the literature and as RATs for another study (RPP).

As shown here, the abstract provides a brief synopsis of the main ingredients of an article in less than 200 words. The general introduction (not psychology introductions) elaborates on the main components of the article (SPL, CPL, GAP) hinted at in the abstract in two to four paragraphs, but explicitly tells readers what it is the authors are going to do in the article (WTD). The literature review section (psychology introductions) will provide a much more extended SPL, CPL, GAP, and RAT (see Chapter 4). The methods section presents the materials, methods, and procedures used in the study. If a critique will be made on methodological grounds, it will revolve around the issue of measurement – measurement of independent and dependent variables and the accuracy and commensurability of measures intended to reflect a particular concept (Harris, 2014). During the act of reading, the code POC should be inserted whenever the reader finds either of the two issues questionable and debatable.

4

So What?

How to Read the General Literature Review, Psychology Introductions, and Results Sections

There is consensus in previous how-to books that the literature review is the most important component of any research paper, from undergraduate theses to PhD dissertations. This point is true of journal articles as well, for it is here that authors review the work of others and make their proposed work relevant to previous works. Furthermore, the critique of the previous works provides a rationale for why our – your – proposed work is necessary and warranted. That is, before we can proffer our own 'knowledge claims' (Vipond, 1996), we must tell readers which authors carried out similar studies and examined similar topics – why our work is sufficiently different and contributes to the knowledge on a given topic.

If the literature is inadequately covered, then the ideas that we present in our papers – knowledge claims, arguments, findings, results – might be framed as being too one-of-a-kind, often ignoring – unwittingly – the work that preceded ours; by doing so, we fail to acknowledge that other scholars have had similar ideas long before. In plain language, undergraduate students and beginning graduate students often try to reinvent the wheel on a given topic. Academic writing, however, should not be conceptualized as wheel invention. Instead, it is more accurate to frame the proposed work as wheel modification. As Vipond (1996, p. 39) advises, do not 'expect to develop your own knowledge claim without first examining and understanding those of other scholars. Claims are seldom completely original; instead, they are connected to, and grow out of, the claims of others.'

One of the elementary mistakes that students make when writing undergraduate research papers and drafts of master's theses is the failure to connect to the work of previous researchers – the literature. Out of deference, a fledgling student might leave out the name of a prominent scholar for fear of contradicting and disagreeing with a 'big name' scholar; or, the omission arises from insufficient reading. Students need to understand that citations are acknowledgements – good or bad – and they are the currency of academic life and business; omitting a relevant name/theorist from the literature review constitutes a slight of the tallest order. Therefore, do not be afraid to critique and disagree. Disagreements are better than omissions, witting and unwitting.

Others who have written books on how to do a literature review have lamented the fact that students simply rehash the work of others in a literature review. We might call this practice making a 'laundry list.' Rudestam and Newton (2001, p. 56) write that:

> many students erroneously believe that the purpose of the literature review is to convince the reader that the writer is knowledgeable about the work of others. Based on this misunderstanding, the literature review may read like a laundry list of previous studies, with sentences or paragraphs beginning with the words "Smith found ... Johnson found ... Jones found ...'

I too made this mistake when I finished my dissertation and submitted a chapter from it to a journal. Both reviewers noted that the literature review read like a laundry list. A laundry list literature review is a simple compendium of facts from previous works, author by author, year by year; it is cumbersome and tedious to read; in a journal article it takes up too much space. Most importantly, a laundry list literature review fails to identity thematically parsimonious points of similarity across the literature. That is why creating a laundry list leads to the laundry list problem.

Previous literature must be organized in some logically connected way. Landrum (2008, p. 96) instructs students to 'group research studies and other types of literature according to common denominators such as qualitative versus quantitative, objectives, methodology, and so forth.' This advice simply means that the laundry list of authors has to be grouped in some principled way. Methodological distinctions are one way to group prior studies; conceptual distinctions are another. However, merely stating what others have said about a topic – author by author, year by year – constitutes only a quarter of a competent literature review. The other quarter entails a thematic and principled summary of previous works. The remaining half entails a thematically connected critique of the previous literature that identifies gaps in the knowledge base, which leads to the rationale for a study.

Summarizing the work of others – the first half of the literature review – is represented by the reading code Summary of Previous Literature (SPL). SPL refers to sentences, paragraphs, or pages that describe a summary of the results from prior studies and works. SPL requires a tremendous amount of condensation, taking complex ideas and reducing them into paragraphs, sentences, and if the author is brilliant enough, one word (see Chapter 8).

How to Read a Literature Review

The location of literature reviews in journal articles differs by discipline. In most psychology journals, the literature review is placed up front as part of the introduction; psychology journals therefore combine a general introduction, where the subcomponents of an article are briefly described, and an extensive literature review into one section. There is a separate section for literature reviews, usually under that very heading, in most sociology, criminology, communication, education, and health journals. No matter where literature reviews are located in a journal article, the work that is done in them is the same: summary of previous work, critique of previous work that highlights a gap in the knowledge, and a rationale of why the proposed – your – work is necessary. Consider how literature reviews are structurally organized.

There are 11 paragraphs in the introduction section of 'Distinguishing juvenile homicide from violent juvenile offending' in DiCataldo and Everett's (2008) article that was published in *International Journal of Offender Therapy and Comparative Criminology*. The first sentence of the first paragraph reads, 'Homicide, particularly by means of firearms, among contemporary American male adolescents has been the focus of intense media coverage, social science research, and moral commentary' (p. 158). This topic sentence provides a succinct yet broad overview of juvenile homicide as a topic. It introduces the reader to what the paper will be about. Moreover, it tells readers that the topic has been addressed by three different stakeholders as well. The rest of the sentences in that paragraph support and illustrate that first topic sentence. The first paragraph and first sentence would be an example of SPL. In the right margin next to this paragraph, the code SPL should be written after the paragraph is read.

The second paragraph begins with the following sentence: 'Juvenile murder is essentially a legal category defined within a state's criminal codes, statutes, and case law' (p. 159). Readers ought to expect that the rest of the sentences that follow this topic sentence will be related to the various definitions of juvenile murder. In fact, the very next sentence reads, 'It is not a diagnostic term, like schizophrenia, or personality disorder' (p. 159). The authors are introducing the distinction between a legal definition of murder and a clinical term used to diagnose offenders' psychological states. Notice that the second sentence supports and elaborates on the first sentence. The rest of the sentences in that second paragraph go on to differentiate between the two categories. So far what we have is SPL, and that code ought to be written in the right margin next to the paragraph. Then the following sentence appears as the last sentence of the second paragraph: 'It remains an empirical question as to whether juvenile murderers are a scientifically valid category apart from their existence as a legal one' (p. 159).

The last sentence clearly does not provide a summary of the previous literature. All of the preceding sentences, in one way or another, have provided support for the ways in which juvenile murder has been conceptualized, defined, and discussed (SPL). The last sentence, however, does not perform that summarizing function. It does suggest that there is a missing element in the existing literature on juvenile homicide: no one has yet to determine if juvenile killers is a 'scientifically valid category.' Another way of describing sentences like that would be to state that they are pointing out a critique

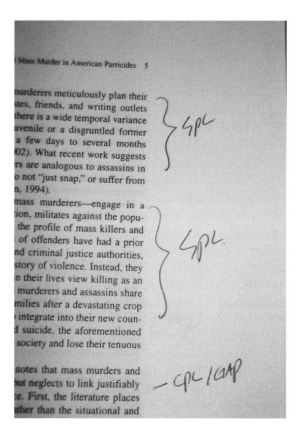

FIGURE 3

(CPL) and a gap (GAP) in the existing literature. There is a gap because no one has addressed that topic; we could also state that that sentence is a Critique of the Previous Literature (CPL) because, again, no one has addressed that question. Next to that sentence, the codes CPL/GAP should be written in the right margin next to that paragraph (Figure 3).

So far, we have examined two paragraphs in one journal article. In those two paragraphs, the authors of the article have summarized the literature into two themes: (1) significance of juvenile murder as a topic; and (2) definition of juvenile murder. In the last sentence of the second paragraph, the possible shortcomings or deficiencies (CPL/GAP) in the literature have been suggested. A CPL provides a critique and points out a limitation contained in previous scholarship. CPL highlights the deficiencies in the existing works on a theoretical, methodological, and analytical level; CPL is conceptually related to GAP since GAP specifically identifies the shortcomings in the literature as well. And notice how those codes, SPL, CPL, and GAP are structurally and logically connected. Before something can be critiqued, the content of that something has to be filled in first. In most, if not all, literature reviews, that is how a critique of the literature is done. The author(s) proffers a body of ideas, theories, and works of previous researchers; if this component is listed one by one, and presented that way in undergraduate research papers, master's theses, PhD dissertations, or journal articles, what we would have is a 'laundry list' – the cardinal sin of any literature review.

But DiCataldo and Everett (2008) do not discuss the literature author by author and year by year in a way that resembles a laundry list. They have synthesized their readings and identified a recurring theme, and structured their literature review along those recurring thematic lines. If you are instructed to synthesize your readings, by definition, you must combine all of your assigned readings and form something new. No one can do that for you. You, the reader and author, must create those thematic categories from the readings you have done. That is what makes the research and writing process – scholarship – creative acts. In addition to developing thematic categories, DiCataldo and Everett (2008) have also begun to subtly hint at the missing dimensions of the existing literature. That is, they have tacitly begun the critique of the previous literature and set up an expectation of the rationale (RAT) for their own work. Structurally, then, SPLs precede CPLs and GAPs. When reading journal articles, CPLs will follow SPLs. Remembering this order is one way to avoid unstructured reading. Readers should understand that ideas in journal articles are structurally and sequentially organized: summaries of literature introduce the reader to a topic in some thematic and principled way; critiques then follow. Again, one cannot begin a critique out of nothing; there has to be something to critique. Film critics cannot – do not – exist if there are no films.

There are other grammatical clues to look for that show CPLs and GAPs are emerging in the text. The third paragraph of 'Distinguishing juvenile homicide' begins with, 'The search for the clinical science behind adolescent murderers is more than a century old.' The sentences that follow clarify in greater detail how that topic has been relevant for at least 100 years, the main feature of previous research being limited sampling. Then the following two sentences appear at the paragraph's end: 'More recent studies have examined larger samples **but** often did not included [sic] control groups of nonhomicide offenders. Some more methodologically sophisticated studies use control groups for comparison purposes **but** elected to use questionable samples of nonviolent delinquents' (p. 159). Notice that phrases like 'more recent studies' and 'some more methodologically sophisticated studies' summarize previous works. In those types of sentences, the first clauses perform the work of SPL; the second clauses do the work of CPL which leads to a GAP. Coordinating the two contrasting ideas are disjunction markers. What do those do in a text?

Pretend for a minute that you are the recipient of the following words from someone you have a crush on: 'I like you; I think you're great. You're sweet; you're funny and really nice ...' Even before I finish the rest of the sentence, I know a lot of readers will know the word that will appear next: '... **BUT** ...' We know because some of us who have lost the parental lottery and have not received the cute gene have heard the painful phrases that follow. In fact, I suspect that when men and women hear a list like that – a series of complimentary assertions that appear independently and without any context or follow a strongly encouraged request for a dialogue ('we should talk') – their gut (not intellect) already senses the bad news to come; the word 'but' confirms the initial suspicion; the actual bad news – 'we should just be friends' – hammers the nail in the coffin.

That disjunction marker – 'but' – coordinates the rejection to come – about why it would be better to be 'just friends' than dating partners. In other words, words like 'but,' 'however,' 'while,' 'albeit,' and 'although' do the work of highlighting and contrasting the consequent from the antecedent. Hence, in the preceding sentences discussed, SPL comes first ('I like you'; 'more recent studies have examined larger samples'; 'some more methodologically sophisticated studies use control groups for comparison purposes'), followed by the CPL/GAP ('we should just be friends'; 'often did not included [sic] control groups of nonhomicide offenders'; 'elected to use questionable samples of nonviolent delinquents'). That a CPL/GAP is on the way is signaled by the appearance of the disjunction marker such as 'but.' In the context of literature reviews, again, SPLs, as a rule, precede CPLs. Grammatical disjunction markers such as 'but' and 'however' are good indicators that the ideas proffered in the first clause or paragraph will be critiqued and qualified in the second. In addition to the structural locations of texts, looking out for grammatical markers that contrast ideas is another way to structure reading so that readers can anticipate critiques.

Does this pattern hold true in other disciplines besides criminology? Does SPL precede CPL and can disjunction markers serve as signs of GAPs to emerge? Consider the following article that J.S. Kim (2001) wrote, 'Daughters-in-law in Korean caregiving families,' published in the *Journal of Advanced Nursing*. The literature review is composed of six paragraphs. The first sentence of the first paragraph of the literature review reads, 'The dynamic of family caregiving and its health consequences may differ by culture because caregiving behaviours may reflect a country's present culture' (p. 401). This sentence does not critique the literature in any way; nor does it declare the results of the author's own studies. Rather, it summarizes the literature on the topic the author has selected. Therefore, the code SPL should be written in the appropriate margin. The second sentence then reads, 'Family caregiving in Korea is influenced by multiple sociocultural factors' (p. 365). Again, the second sentence elaborates on the main topic hinted at in the first sentence. The first paragraph could be thematically coded as 'why DIL caregiver' to reflect what the entire paragraph is about. The remaining paragraphs go on to explain why daughters-in-law (DIL) in Korea have to be caregivers to elderly parents on their husband's side.

So why do daughters-in-law have to be caregivers in a Korean context? Kim (2001) explains in the literature review section that in Korean culture, heavily influenced by the Confucian principle of filial piety, the eldest son must assume responsibility for taking care of his elderly parents; the wife of the husband, by default, takes on the role of being a caregiver. Kim writes that normative expectations and social pressures compel daughters-in-law to accept their gendered role as caregivers. This background information on the social organization of families in Korea, as well as how industrial and social changes have altered the roles of women in society, and the context of caregiving are covered in the six paragraphs of the literature review. The previous literature on DILs as caregivers in a Western context suggests that they experience the highest level of negative health outcomes. But, as noted, it is not enough to simply summarize the literature; there must be shortcomings in the literature that warrant Kim's study of DIL as caregivers in Korea. What is Kim's CPL?

The first sentence of the last paragraph of the literature review states the following: 'In Korea, no study has been conducted to differentiate between blood-tied and affinal relationships' (p. 402). That is, while DILs as caregivers have been examined from a Western perspective, DILs as caregivers in a Korean context have been absent. That criticism is a valid one, for there may be cultural, social, and economic reasons why caregiving may be different in a Korean – or any other national and cultural – context. Now, notice how that CPL is rehearsed in the introduction. The following sentences appear in the second paragraph of the introduction:

> Previous Western studies have reported that DIL caregivers experience the greatest adverse health consequences of parent caregiving [citation omitted] and have found that in-law caregivers provide less help to their PILs (parents-in-law) than blood-tied caregivers [citations omitted] ... Although DIL caregivers have comprised a significant portion of caregivers and have an increased risk status in Korea, DILs as caregivers in Korea have not been studied extensively and systematically ... However, no study has been conducted of the health outcomes of DIL caregivers who care for impaired older people in the context of Korean culture. (p. 400)

Notice that the SPL precedes the CPL: previous research has found that DILs provide less help to parents-in-law (PIL) than those related by blood. From an evolutionary perspective, those findings would be logical and expected. However, that assumption cannot be extended to Korea for cultural reasons (i.e., Confucianism). That claim is the basis of Kim's CPL of the prior literature on caregiving. Again, SPLs precede CPLs. Furthermore, disjunction markers portend the contrastive point that follows the antecedent. While readers are not led to see how the CPL emerges from the SPL in the literature review, that pattern does occur in the introduction. What answer would Kim provide if we asked the 'So what?' question? Consider the next sentence: 'As little is known about this topic, a study which explores the health outcomes of DIL caregivers who care for impaired PIL (parents-in-law) in the sociocultural context of Korea is necessary' (p. 400). That sentence would constitute the RAT for her paper. Kim provides only one RAT, but there are several more RATs she could have provided that would bolster the significance of her work.

For example, as two non-blood-related family members, the potential for violence increases between DIL and mothers-in-law as the evolutionary rule of nepotism predicts. For DIL, living amidst husbands' family members as part of a patrilocal residence structure would place them at risk of violence, at least according to an evolutionary theory of violence. Second, as cohabitants within the same household, or as a result of prolonged contact as a result of caregiving, there is potential for domestic discord between mothers- and daughters-in-law, thereby increasing the risk of expressive violence. Third, DILs as caregivers have the potential to be parricide offenders, as ordinary caregiving tasks turn into elder abuse that turn fatal. From a criminological perspective, there are numerous reasons why a study of DILs and caregiving in a Korean context may be significant. From a nursing and health perspective, readers are proffered one. But the one RAT that is provided suffices to convince readers why a study of DILs as caregivers in Korea is necessary.

The literature review in Hu and Ma's (2010) article, 'Mentoring and student persistence in college: A study of the Washington State Achievers Program,' published in *Innovative Higher Education*, is five paragraphs long. The first two sentences of the first paragraph of the introduction read as follows: 'Policy makers, institutional administrators, and researchers have been interested in student persistence in college over decades [citations omitted]. One of the best-known models on college student persistence is the integration model proposed by Tinto' (p. 330). Both sentences introduce readers to a broad SPL. The first paragraph is spent reviewing the prior work that Tinto has done; Tinto's work constitutes the SPL in the first paragraph. The phrase 'integration model' would aptly summarize what this paragraph is about in a thematically concise way; 'Tinto model' would also work, for the first term originates from Tinto.

In the second paragraph, Hu and Ma (2010) discuss alternative models of student persistence, and their strengths and weaknesses; in the third paragraph, the authors go on to discuss the role that faculty mentoring plays in student persistence. In addition to the SPL codes that ought to be written in the right margin, the appropriate one- or two-word phrases should be written in the left margin as thematic codes. Then in the fourth paragraph, the following sentences appear:

> Several studies have examined the relationship between mentoring and student persistence, and overall results indicate that mentoring has a significant and positive impact on student persistence [citations omitted]. However, these studies have focused on the impact of a mentoring program without examining the specific aspects of mentoring. Consequently, they have not investigated how student background characteristics are related to different aspects of mentoring and, subsequently, how different aspects of mentoring influence student persistence. (p. 331)

Then, in the last two sentences of the last paragraph of the literature review, the following sentences appear:

> The mentoring aspects of the WSA [Washington State Achievers] Program reflect the domains or features identified by Freeman (1999) as well as Nora and Crisp (2007). However, it has been unclear how different mentoring elements of the WSA Program contributed to student persistence, which was the focus of this study. (pp. 331–2)

As can be seen here, SPL occurs before CPL, repeating the pattern noted in the literature reviews in other disciplines. Similarly, the disjunction marker 'however' again portends the CPL to follow the SPL. Although there may be other techniques that scholars have used to summarize and critique the literature, I have found that the structural organization of texts and the grammatical markers that indicate conceptual transitions are good heuristic devices to employ during the act of reading. Thus, without even elaborating on the content of the sentences, their structural location in the text, the grammatical clues proffered, and by examining only the form of the sentences, readers can discern that the second sentence critiques the first – pushes against the ideas contained in the first sentence. Understanding the work that sentences and paragraphs perform in a journal article is the first step in organizing the information that one reads in the literature. Thus, without even reading the content of the sentence, we know that the sentences in the literature review which begin with declarative assertions such as, 'Several studies have examined ...' 'The mentoring aspects of the WSA ...' 'According to Tinto ...' will be a summary of previous works (SPL). The disjunction marker 'however' intimates that the rest of the words to follow will push against the preceding SPL. Similarly, sentences that begin with words such as 'although,' 'despite,' 'yet,' 'unfortunately,' 'regrettably,' and 'sadly' connect the SPL and CPL by putting the disjunction marker first, but still abide by the SPL→CPL format. That is why SPL, CPL, and GAP are logically connected. Although only heuristic, the reading codes represent simple guidelines to follow when reading social science journal articles.

Hu and Ma's (2010) critique of the student persistence literature (CPL) is that prior researchers have failed to delve into 'how student background characteristics are related to different aspects of mentoring,' and how that omission has led researchers to overlook other aspects of mentoring. Furthermore, Hu and Ma (2010) charge that previous researchers have neglected to examine how 'different mentoring elements of the WSA Program contributed to student persistence.' In other words, Hu and Ma reviewed the literature on student persistence and noticed that there were missing components in the literature. Those missing elements constitute the GAPs in the literature. The existence of those GAPs serves as a rationale for why Hu and Ma's work was necessary (RAT). That is why they carried out their study.

Some journals (and authors and disciplines) organize summaries and critiques into separate and distinct sections. For instance, Dixon and Linz (2000) organize the summary of the literature of their article on 'Race and the misrepresentation of victimization on local television news,' published in *Communication Research*, into the following thematic categories: (1) overemphasis on White victimization; (2) indices of victimization; (3) intergroup comparisons of victims; (4) interrole comparisons of victimization; (5) utility of intergroup and interrole measures; (6) interreality comparisons. Again, notice what the authors have not done. They have not listed the literature author by author and year by year in the manner of a laundry list. They have organized the voluminous literature on race, media, and crime into the afore-mentioned six categories, in a way that is meaningful for what they aim to do in their work. Dixon and Linz (2000, pp. 553–4) go on to provide a separate section for the limitations of previous literature section: 'This section attempts to overcome several of the limitations of prior works that examined race and victimization. In this section, we lay out three limitations of this prior research and how this addresses them.' One could even anticipate what the criticism might be based on the way the existing literature is organized and discussed. This type of a structural format makes reading and organizing voluminous amounts of information easier, for readers are spared from acting like textual detectives. Even this type of format, however, follows the general rule stipu-lated here: SPL, then CPL. Again, that is because, before we can critique a body of work, the reader has to know what that body of work is so the critique can be meaningful. The GAP emerges from this process.

GAPs are conceptually related to RATs. The deficiencies in the present state of knowledge justify and warrant a study that will remedy the missing gap in the knowledge base – that is the rationale for why a study is necessary. So if someone asks, 'So what? Why should anyone care about your work?', the answer ought to be a derivative of CPL and GAP. Thus, if someone asks you why any-one should care about your work (senior thesis, master's thesis, or dissertation), your hypothetical response should be something like the following:

> My study is worth doing because: (1) few have done it; (2) others who have done the type of work have used incorrect measures, used the wrong statis-tical tests, or incorrectly defined the problem; (3) they have made little progress beyond what the seminal theorists have done.

In journal articles, the answers to the 'So what?' question come in three to five carefully argued RATs.

Dixon and Linz (2000) list three answers to the 'So what?' question that is logically connected to CPL and GAP. (1) Previous studies have used one mea-sure. This sentence would be an example of CPL/GAP. So how will this gap be remedied? 'This study uses multiple indicators' (p. 554). The use of multiple indicators is RAT #1. (2) 'Very few studies have analyzed portrayals of Latinos on television news.' This sentence would be an example of CPL/GAP. So how will this gap be remedied? The current work analyzes Latinos. Analysis of Latinos on television is RAT #2. (3) No one has examined Los Angeles television news. This sentence would be an example of CPL/GAP. So how will this gap be remedied? Our current work examines Los Angeles television news where a lot of Latinos live. This answer is RAT #3.The three GAPs in the literature and their proposed remedies function as the RAT – the rationale for the study. In a proper literature review one must review and summarize the literature (SPL), critique the literature (CPL) by finding shortcomings and deficiencies in the literature (GAPs); and the remedy of those gaps constitutes the rationale for the proposed study (RAT): SPL→CPL→GAP→RAT. A competently done literature review – not a laundry list – generally follows the format outlined above.

Rudestam and Newton (2001) write that a literature review is more than a simple list of previous works. As argued here, that is only half of a literature review. A competently done literature review ought to transport the reader to the destination before arriving. In Rudestam and Newton's (2001, p. 58) words, 'by the end of the literature review, the reader should be able to conclude that "yes, of course, this is the exact study that needs to be done at this time to move knowledge in this field a little further along".' That 'yes' moment occurs because the SPL→RAT process unfolds in a logical, thematic, and anticipatable way; and advances in disciplines do not occur by leaps and bounds; they occur incrementally, one study at a time. Each study modifies the wheel little by little. When readers finish reading the SPL, CPL, and GAP, they should be able to anticipate the RAT, the hypothesis to be tested, or argument being made. When students are writing, the logical structure of their papers ought to follow along the preceding lines so that readers can expect and anticipate the next item from the previous one.

For example, White, Bates, and Buyske's (2001) article that examines the delinquent trajectories of adolescents into adulthood, published in the *Journal of Abnormal Psychology*, tests two hypotheses:

On the basis of previous studies of childhood-to-adolescence persistence, we hypothesized that three different trajectories would be identified ... we also hypothesized that adolescence-limited and adolescence-to-adulthood-persistent delinquents would differ on selected measures of neuropsychological functioning, personality risk, and environmental risk. (p. 601)

How did the authors arrive at these two hypotheses? The key theorist in this area is Terrie Moffitt (1993a, 1993b), a developmental psychologist who claims that delinquency is temporary for most delinquents while for some it persists into adulthood (SPL). The authors organize the SPL into three themes: (1) neuropsychological dysfunction; (2) personality; (3) environmental adversity. White et al. (2001) go on to write,

Yet, little is currently known about the utility of this typology for differentiating adolescence-limited from adolescence-to-adulthood-persistent delinquency ... **Although** neuropsychological functioning and personality characteristics have been found to differentiate early-onset from late-onset delinquents, few studies have examined their ability to differentiate those individuals who persist in delinquency beyond adolescence from those who do not. (p. 601; emphasis added)

White et al. summarize the literature (SPL), point out the limitations of previous works (CPL) and identify a deficiency in the literature (GAP); and by pointing out the shortcoming in the previous literature, the authors have provided an implicit RAT for why their work is necessary and warranted. If someone were to ask them, 'So what?' they could answer by stating that no one knows the 'utility of this typology' and that 'few studies are able to differentiate life-course-persistent offenders from adolescent-limited offenders.' Those answers to the 'So what?' question are their way of remedying the GAP in the literature. From this logical chain of reasoning, the hypothesis emerges. The emergence of the hypothesis is not an act of magic – out of the blue – for authors carefully set up the reader to anticipate the hypothesis, and to see the logic of their reasoning by introducing her to the literature (SPL), its limitations and criticisms (CPL), and shortcomings (GAP). The hypothesis follows naturally and inevitably from the way the authors have crafted and organized their ideas. That is why, by the end of a literature review, the reader is able to 'conclude that "yes, of course, this is the exact study that needs to be done at this time to move knowledge in this field a little further along"' (Rudestam & Newton, 2001, p. 58).

How to Read the Results Section

Results sections are probably the easiest to read, for authors simply lay out their main findings. In 'Urban black violence: The effect of male joblessness and family disruption,' Sampson (1987, p. 377) reports the following results, published in *American Journal of Sociology*: 'while male joblessness has little or no impact on crime, it has the strongest overall effect on family disruption, which in turn is the strongest predictor of black violence.' An assertion like the preceding one in the results section constitutes a 'knowledge claim' and should be treated as such by marking in the right margin ROF (Result of Findings). ROFs describe the primary results of the article being read. That particular finding is significant given the author's summary and critique of the previous literature – previous theories that have explained black criminality in the US as a function of a subculture that condones and promotes violence. Sampson is arguing against such views in this article.

The ROFs are the most significant, accessible, and visible pieces of information in social science journal articles for the simple reason that they are found in the abstract, results, and discussion and conclusion sections of most, if not all, social science journal articles. They tend to be repeated at least three times in the course of a journal article. The main ROFs are what need to be marked, highlighted, and noted, for they are the golden nuggets of journal articles; they are what the article is 'about'; the ROFs contain the central claims of authors – the citable points; ROFs will also become the SPLs of the papers that students write. So what are some of the notable ROFs from the articles we have examined thus far? DiCataldo and Everett (2008, p. 167) report in their results section (published in the *International Journal of Offender Therapy and Comparative Criminology*) that 'the non-homicide group had more significant delinquent histories than the homicide group on a number of the delinquency variables.' Such a ROF is significant because it is counterintuitive and also supports previous literature. Pritchard and Hughes (1997, pp. 58, 60) report in their results, published in *Journal of Communication*, that 'the race of a homicide victim accounted for almost all of the predictive power of race,' and that the 'most consistent predictor of newsworthiness was whether the victim was a child or a senior.' The ROFs are noteworthy because the authors are showing patterns in newspaper coverage that others have simply assumed.

J.S. Kim (2001) reports her findings, published in the *Journal of Advanced Nursing*, that relationship type was not an important predictor of caregivers' health, that daughters and DIL fared similarly to one another. Those findings are significant because one would expect non-consanguineous relatives to experience more health problems when caring for the family members by marriage. Hu and Ma (2010) report their findings, published in *Innovative Higher Education*, that the educational aspirations of college students are salient factors that explain the effectiveness of faculty mentors and student persistence. They also report that students who have at least one parent with a college degree are more likely to seek out mentors for support and encouragement. That finding is noteworthy because the very students who may need the most encouragement and support (first generation college students whose parents never attended college) may be the least likely ones to seek them out.

All of the significant and relevant – for your paper's aims – ROFs ought to be highlighted, underlined, or made salient in some way; the code ROF should be written in the right margin so that even if the reader wants to go back and look up the main findings several months later, she can look at the ROF code and know exactly what it is that she is looking at. Students should not have to re-read an article in order to figure out what the paper is 'about.' Instead, they should be able to look at the most important parts of journal articles – highlighted portions – and figure out exactly what claims are being made by the authors. The ROFs are also significant because they will need to be synthesized and integrated into the student's own literature review. The ROFs of the journal articles that students read will become the SPLs of their papers.

Transitioning from ROF to SPL: Making the Quarter Turn

As I have shown here, the reading codes are meant to facilitate critical reading by having students understand the work that sentences and paragraphs perform in a particular type of text, the social science journal article. By writing the pertinent reading codes in the right margins, the readers are actively reading by summarizing (SPL), critiquing (CPL), identifying short-comings (GAP), and cultivating points of critique (POC). Simply put, the general instructions that previous scholars have proffered to 'read critically' and 'think critically' have simply been condensed into operational codes that could be deployed during the act of reading. When it comes time for students to write their own literature reviews, for a research paper, thesis, or disser-tation, they have to reproduce in their papers what they have read others do in those social science journal articles. The reading codes are meant to help students in the writing process by actively and critically engaging with texts – precisely by summarizing, critiquing, identifying gaps, and cultivat-ing their own unique contributions to the literature during the act of reading. For example, let's say that an undergraduate senior is writing an honors thesis on personality and crime, and she has found 30 journal articles that have been published on that topic within the last 10 years. How should she organize her literature review?

First, the ROFs from the 30 articles she has read will become SPLs of her paper. That is because the 30 articles she found on personality and crime while searching Psychinfo or any other database constitutes – is – the previ-ous literature. The authors of those 30 articles will have read the seminal works of other researchers in the field, and the works they have read became the SPLs of their articles. The 30 authors identified CPLs and GAPs and proposed to remedy those GAPs in the literature (RAT) by conducting origi-nal studies. The results of those original studies constituted the ROFs of their papers – these ROFs become the SPLs of your (the student) paper. Therefore, the first step involves looking through the 30 articles and figuring out what common denominators exist in all of her ROFs because those ROFs will become her SPLs. Again, Landrum (2008) tells us to 'group research studies and other types of literature according to common denominators such as qualitative versus quantitative, objectives, methodology' and so on. Second, the said student will have to look for common patterns that could be collapsed into several themes. Once students read enough previous works, they will begin to 'see' thematic patterns in the literature. The left margin thematic codes, once entered into the Reading Code Organization Sheet (RCOS), will enable students to visually inspect those themes in the previous literature. What students cannot do is list the 30 authors one by one; then a laundry list problem is created. There is a way to mine the 30 articles you have read to assist you in your writing process.

Our hypothetical student who is writing her paper on personality and crime can begin by looking through the 30 articles and scanning the right margins and identifying all SPLs. She would then examine that sentence and/or paragraph and write a sufficiently broad theme or a word in the left margin of the printed articles. For example, in DiCataldo and Everett's (2008) article on juvenile murder there should be three words that summarize the three paragraphs we used as excerpts: (1) significance; (2) definition; (3) time – or something along those lines. For the Dixon and Linz (2000) article, there should be six words/phrases that thematically summarize the paragraphs and sentences: (1) White emphasis; (2) victimization indices; (3) comparisons; (4) intergroup/interrole; (5) interreality. Thematic code insertions can be done at the same time that reading codes are inserted, on the first act of reading, or saved for later. Doing both simultaneously, however, requires practice. Until the reader is familiar enough with the reading codes, and comfortable enough with the act of reading, the left margin insertions ought to be done after the first act of reading. When trying to come up with ways of organizing your own literature review, the thematic codes and summaries ought to serve as a guide in the preparation of your paper. Use the way previous SPLs are organized from your reading of the 30 articles as a way of framing and guiding your own SPL from the ROFs. Students will begin to see a pattern in the prior literature between articles number 12 and 15; once students have read between 12 and 15 journal articles, they will begin to understand the debate, notice the recurring themes in the literature, as well as important theorists in the area. The most frequently occurring thematic SPL codes are a hint that those themes should be included in the student's literature review. We might call this practice turning the SPL a quarter turn. Why reinvent the wheel?

The second step in the writing process involves coming up with a critique of the previous literature so that you can justify your paper on personality and crime. Your research question is shaped by the shortcomings in the literature; your paper is attempting to remedy those gaps that exist in the literature. You do not 'just' write a research paper or 'just' make a claim of your own. Your 'take' on a topic arises from what is missing in the literature. You need to be able to answer the 'So what?' question. How do you go about finding limitations and deficiencies in previous literature? Go through your 30 journal articles and identify all the GAPs. What patterns exist in your GAP collection? What POC can you develop based on those GAPs? POC is a deficiency in the articles you have read or the literature in general that you could use as a way of remedying a deficiency in the literature. POC is easily developed with experience; that is because POC is developed and refined over time – through years of continuous reading. First-time graduate students and upper-class undergraduates do not yet have the experience of cultivating POCs when they embark on their research papers. There is a way, however, for beginners to exploit their reading codes to cultivate their POC.

Students should consult books and articles on developing a critique of existing works. For example, Crasswell and Poore (2012) instruct students to follow their hunch as they read. Lipson (2005) advises undergraduates to pay attention to questions that have not been asked or pursued in readings; those shortcomings, he advises, should be explored in one's undergraduate thesis. A much more systematic and heuristic way of critiquing social science journal articles is to examine the following (see Harris, 2014): (1) definition – its lack of consensus and ambiguity; (2) measurement – its inconsistency, variable choice, and selection; (3) causal relationships between variables; (4) ethics; (5) policy implications. Harris's (2014) book provides an excellent introduction to the typical ways that social science journal articles can be critiqued. There is one more way that students can develop a critique for their own research purposes.

Go through the 30 articles again and scan for CPLs. As mentioned earlier, CPL is a critique of SPL. On what grounds did the previous authors – authors of the 30 articles you will have read – critique the SPL? That is, are there common denominators in the way that the authors of the 30 articles on personality and crime have CPLed the SPL? Usually, the answer is yes. Use those existing themes to cultivate your own POC. Moreover, look at the right margins again and identify all the Recommendations for Future Works (RFWs). RFWs are signposts to the GAPs in the literature. That is why the authors put them in their conclusions – because there is still a GAP in the literature that needs to be remedied. RFWs, along with patterns and trends in the way SPL is CPLed, are a good way to mine for one's own unique way of organizing a literature review. The RFWs are shortcuts to formulating your own GAPs. Using that existing pattern others have used as a way of framing your own paper might be called 'making a quarter turn.' Such turns do not invert or subvert the established ideas, theories, and critiques in paradigm-shifting ways; you are simply turning the SPL and CPL just enough to be different from previous studies while justifying the necessity of your own proposed study. That is why a careful reading of the discussion and conclusion sections is important.

5

Becoming a Part of the Scholarly Community

How to Read the Discussion and Conclusion

In previous chapters, I noted that one of the elementary mistakes students make when writing undergraduate research papers and drafts of graduate theses is the failure to connect to the works of previous researchers. Regrettably, this problem is not unique to students; freshly minted PhDs and even seasoned academics fail to connect their papers to the relevant literature. I am no exception. I too have made this error, and continue to make it because I have not read sufficiently or widely. In previous chapters, I also argued that connecting to the work of others in the literature review entails doing two things: (1) summarizing the work that others have done (SPL); and (2) identifying shortcomings in the current state of the literature as part of a critique (CPL, GAP). Once previous works are discussed and critiqued, students have set up a rationale (RAT) for why their proposed work (e.g., honors thesis, master's thesis, and PhD dissertation) is warranted and necessary. The proposed work will be necessary because it will remedy the knowledge gap that exists in the literature. Once you – the student – are able to defend why your proposed study is necessary, you can begin the data collection process, analyze the data, and present the results of your study as part of an undergraduate research paper, undergraduate honors thesis, master's thesis, and PhD dissertation. As I have argued in this book, social science journal articles that students have to read also follow the aforementioned general format (SPL→CPL→GAP→RAT). After authors have critiqued and provided a rationale for their studies, they have to provide a description of the data and methods used to analyze them. After the data and methods are introduced, authors present their findings in the results section. After the results are presented, then what? In most, if not all, social science journal articles, the authors provide readers with a discussion and/or conclusion section. This chapter teaches students how to read them.

In the discussion section, the Results of Findings (ROFs) are interpreted and explained in the context of the previous literature; ROFs from a study are significant given the author's summary and critique of the previous literature. In the results section, the findings are generally stated, without additional commentary or elaboration. If the literature review transports readers into the history of a discipline and a topic by bringing the past – previous scholars – to the present, the current study – then the discussion and conclusion take the findings from present research into the past and back to the future. In the literature review, the past is made relevant to the present by pointing out the limitations of previous works, which the current work attempts to overcome; in the discussion section, the present is made relevant to the past by interpreting current results in the context of past findings; moreover, the deficiencies in the current work are made relevant for other scholars who may want to remedy those gaps in the future. The discussion section thereby transports readers across three time periods – past, present, and future – by interpreting the present in the context of the past, and through self-reflexive criticism that sets up the RAT for future research.

For example, Glatthorn and Joyner (2005) instruct their writers (readers) to ask themselves what the study 'means' when writing discussion sections. To do so, they provide helpful questions to follow when writing – and I would argue reading – one's own discussion section: what is the 'relationship of the current study to prior research?' and what are the 'theoretical implications' of the study? Are there insights that the researcher could proffer? Are there unanticipated results that need to be reconciled and resolved? As Jordan and Zanna (1999) note, discussions can be 'particularly interesting when the results did not work out exactly as the researchers anticipated.' Furthermore, what are the limitations of the current research and what recommendations could be made for future and further research? If a competently executed literature review demonstrates its debt to the works of previous researchers and scholars by building upon their research, then the discussion and conclusion sections also perform a similar function by tethering the results of the current study to the past. That is why knowledge claims grow out of the claims of others: they are conceptually, methodologically, and temporally bound to the cyclical and historical character of academic scholarship. Knowledge claims do not – cannot – begin *ab initio*. Those types of questions that previous scholars have instructed writers to contemplate while writing discussion sections are also applicable to students who are reading journal articles. In this chapter, reading codes that are particularly related to discussions and conclusions (i.e., RCL, RTC, RFW, RPP) are taught and discussed.

How to Read the Discussion Section

If there are minute differences in where the literature reviews are located in social science journal articles, discussion and conclusion sections almost always appear toward the end of an article – for the same reason that introductions have to appear at the beginning of an article. In the section below, selected paragraphs from discussion sections are reproduced in order to teach students how to read the discussions and conclusions. To describe the function of the sentences in the discussion section, and for accessibility, clarity, and ease of reference, each sentence has been numbered consecutively. There are ten paragraphs in the discussion section of 'Distinguishing juvenile homicide from violent juvenile offending' in DiCataldo and Everett's (2008) article published in *International Journal of Offender Therapy and Comparative Criminology*. The first paragraph of the discussion begins the following way:

(1) This study set out to determine if adolescent homicide offenders could indeed be distinguished from a sample of violent nonhomicide perpetrators. (2) The overall findings contradict the predominant portrayals of adolescent homicide perpetrators in popular media outlets as the clinically distinguishable super-predator or cold psychopath compared with violent nonhomicide perpetrators, many of whom had been charged or convicted of murder. (3) In this study, the nonhomicide participants proved more problematic on many of the variables of analysis. (4) They often began their delinquent careers earlier, had significantly greater numbers of total offenses, and had more violent offenses. (5) The nonhomicide participants often had less stable early childhood histories, with more frequent placements out of the home and more frequent sibling delinquency. (6) They also reported being more likely to use knives in crimes of violence than the homicide group.

The first sentence of the first paragraph of the discussion tells readers the main research question that the authors have asked and attempted to answer in their paper. Sentences like it describe What They (the authors) Did (WTDD). WTDD is a logical and historical cognate of WTD that appears in the past tense in discussions and conclusions. Thus, there is temporal symmetry between WTD and WTDD, for authors instruct readers what they will do in the introduction and what they have done in the discussion and conclusion. The reading code WTDD should be written in the right margin next to that sentence. The next sentence interprets and contextualizes the primary results of the findings (ROF) from their study to the broader literature and culture.

The word 'contradict' explicitly informs readers that DiCataldo and Everett's ROF was inconsistent with the popular notion of what it means to be a juvenile killer. Such sentences are best represented by the code RTC (Results To the Contrary), and that code ought to be written in the right margin. The rest of the sentences in that paragraph go on to elaborate on the ROFs from their study: that nonhomicide offenders were more problematic on several measures; they started criminal careers earlier than the homicide offender group, and had less stable lives at home. In the very next paragraph, DiCataldo and Everett (2008) note that the nonhomicide group had anger control issues and bad memories of their parents as well.

If the code RTC describes the way the ROFs contradict the findings from the literature, Results that are Consistent with the Literature (RCL) describe findings that corroborate and support results from previous studies. Thus, sentences like:

> The homicide perpetrators' more frequent reports that they were intoxicated at the time of their deadly violent acts are consistent with recent research by Dolan and Smith (2001), who also reported that their sample of juvenile homicide offenders were more likely to report that they had abused alcohol at the time of their offenses than the nonhomicide offenders.

and:

> The homicide participants' greater exposure to guns at home within their personal histories as a predisposing factor to their later homicidal acts is consistent with a recent report by Bingenheimer, Brennan and Earls (2005), who concluded that being exposed to firearm violence nearly doubled the probability that an adolescent would commit a serious violent act in the subsequent 2 years. (DiCataldo & Everett, 2008, p. 170)

in these third and fourth paragraphs nestle their findings in the context and work of previous researchers. That is, rather than simply presenting their findings as new knowledge claims, they bind their ROFs within the context of work that others have already done. By doing so, DiCataldo and Everett (2008) join the community of researchers whose work corroborates a particular finding; they participate in the construction and reproduction of knowledge in the scholarly community – their claims become tied to the claims of others. Although their primary findings are RTC, other facets of their findings are consistent with the literature (RCL) on the topic, and next to those types of sentences, the code RCL should be written in the right margin (Figure 4).

So far, the authors have described how the findings from their research contradict and support the work that others have done. By linking their work to those of others, they are executing the very advice that writers like Glatthorn and Joyner (2005) have provided: answering questions like, 'What is the relationship of the current study to prior research?', and what are the 'theoretical implications' of the study? The codes RCL and RTC describe two interpretive possibilities for ROFs of a study, and by elaborating on the relationship of the current ROFs to past ROFs the current findings are made

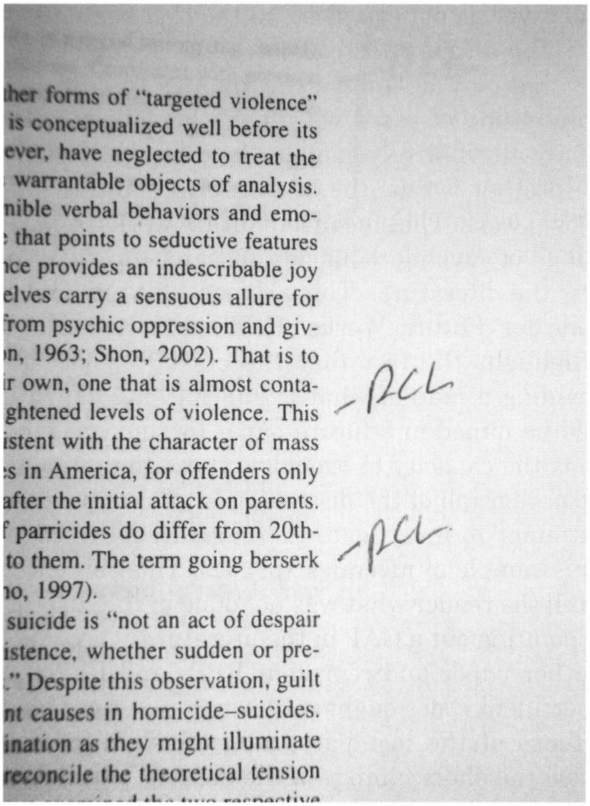

ther forms of "targeted violence"
is conceptualized well before its
ever, have neglected to treat the
warrantable objects of analysis.
nible verbal behaviors and emo-
: that points to seductive features
ice provides an indescribable joy
elves carry a sensuous allure for
rom psychic oppression and giv-
n, 1963; Shon, 2002). That is to
r own, one that is almost conta-
ghtened levels of violence. This   ̶ РСL
istent with the character of mass
s in America, for offenders only
after the initial attack on parents.
f parricides do differ from 20th-
to them. The term going berserk   ̶ рСL
io, 1997).
suicide is "not an act of despair
istence, whether sudden or pre-
." Despite this observation, guilt
nt causes in homicide–suicides.
ination as they might illuminate
reconcile the theoretical tension

FIGURE 4

meaningful and situated in the community of scholars who have carried out similar and related works. Although DiCataldo and Everett (2008) do not discuss the theoretical implications of their work, they do address the policy implications of their findings. They go on to critique the legislative changes that have occurred in the US, which seek to treat adolescent killers like adults in the criminal justice system; such policies, they argue, are aimed at the wrong population, for their ROFs would indicate that nonhomicide offenders are much more psycho-socially problematic than homicide offenders. Again, by teasing out the implications of their research and findings for public policy, the authors make their research meaningful in the larger social context: they are able to contextualize their findings and make them relevant in the ongoing debate about crime and punishment; they are able to critique a social policy that may be targeting the wrong group and causing undue harm; more importantly, they can substantiate such criticisms based on empirical research. Those types of implications – theoretical, conceptual, methodological, policy – are teased out and pursued in the discussion section.

Their work, however, is not complete. In the first sentence of paragraph five of the discussion, the authors write 'There exist a number of selection biases within this study that may account for the findings' (p. 170). They point out that 'a differential processing of cases within the juvenile justice system may be operating that may alternatively explain the differences identified within this study' (p. 170). In other words, the authors are pointing out shortcomings – GAPs – in their own work. That means, in future works, someone could address those shortcomings of juvenile homicide research to overcome a GAP in the current state of the literature. Those types of sentences would illustrate Recommendations for Future Works (RFW) and Relevant Point to Pursue (RPP). RFWs highlight the fact that the current paper is incomplete; the authors are providing a map of what is still missing (GAP) in the literature. Such POCs could be mined in a future paper by someone who is interested in the topic, and has the capacity to overcome those limitations. In the first sentence of the last paragraph of the discussion, a similar sentence appears: 'This study did not attempt to investigate the motivations or circumstances of the homicides for this sample of juveniles' (p. 172). This sentence again is a POC, for the authors tell the reader what was not done in the current paper; logically, the authors are pointing out a GAP in the literature. Those GAPs could be used as POCs in another paper and represent RPPs and RFWs. Next to relevant sentences, the pertinent codes ought to be written in the right margin.

The last sentence of the last paragraph of the discussion is even more explicit about how the shortcomings of the current paper can be remedied:

> Future research with this sample will progress toward a finer-grained, within-group analysis of the homicide perpetrators, coding the multidimensional contextual features of their acts of homicide by looking at the physical setting of the homicide, the interactional and historical relationships with the victims, the means and methods of homicide, the posthomicide behavior of the perpetrators, and the legal outcomes' (p. 172)

In other words, the RFWs just mentioned illustrate the missing elements in the literature on juvenile homicide (GAPs) – they need to be addressed in the future. The code RFW should be written in the right margin of paper. That is five POCs and GAPs the authors have provided in one sentence alone. That such GAPs and POCs are already contained in the articles being read is the reason why reading should not be treated as a secondary activity. The components of a future paper – most importantly GAPs – are already embedded in the current work. Writers do not necessarily have to come up with 'new ideas' because they are already buried in the readings. Future writers just have to know how to find them during the act of reading. RFWs represent POCs and CPLs/GAPs that are already embedded in the discussion and conclusion sections that should be used as a resource for students who are reading social science journal articles.

There are seven paragraphs that make up the discussion section, in addition to the two paragraphs on limitations and suggestions for future research, and one conclusion paragraph in E.H. Kim et al.'s (2014) article on 'Hwa-byung among middle-aged Korean women: Family relationships, gender-role attitudes, and self-esteem' published in *Health Care for Women International*. In all, ten paragraphs are spent on the discussion and conclusion. The notable sentences that we want to examine in greater detail from the discussion section begin the following way:

> (1) Our main purposes for this study were twofold: (a) to examine how family relationship problems, attitudes toward women's roles, and self-esteem were related to HB [hwa-byung, Korean anger syndrome], and (b) to test gender-role attitudes as a moderator for the relationship between family relationship problems and HB. (2) Our study was one of the first attempts to empirically examine these variables in a nonclinical sample of Korean women. (3) Only three demographic variables, including single/never married status, education status, and hours husband worked were found to be positively associated with HB ... (6) In terms of hours that husbands worked, we speculated that the more the husband worked, the less he is available for emotional support and help. (7) This result is similar to Kim and Kim's (1994) findings that emotional support of the husband was positively related to married women's mental well-being. (p. 505)

Sentences #1 and #2, again, describe what the authors did in their study. Consequently, the reading code WTDD is most appropriate and should be written in the right margin next to those sentences. Sentence #3 reports the significant results of their study, so the reading code ROF should be written in the right margin next to that sentence. Sentence #6 reports a significant ROF from their study, and speculates as to its causes. In sentence #7, Kim et al. again interpret their ROF and contextualize it against the broader literature. They note that their results are 'similar to Kim and Kim's (1994) findings.' The phrase 'similar to' means that their results are consistent with Kim and Kim's (1994) findings. Therefore, the reading code RCL should be written in the right margin. Throughout the rest of the discussion and conclusion section, Kim et al. go on to interpret and contextualize their ROF against the literature.

Consider the following sentences in the fourth paragraph of Kim et al.'s discussion:

> (1) We found that as women endorsed egalitarian and profeminist attitudes, HB symptoms increased. (2) This result is consistent with that of Choi and colleagues (2009), in which individualistic and less traditional family values were positively associated with HB. (3) It differs from other studies, however,

where HB patients in psychiatry and primary care settings noted strong commitments to traditional feminine roles. (p. 506)

Notice the repeating pattern in the discussion again. The authors repeat their main ROF, and then go on to contextualize their findings relative to previous research. For example, sentence #2 interprets sentence #1 (ROF) against the findings of Choi et al., which indicates that Kim et al.'s findings are consistent with Choi et al.'s (RCL). That is to say that HB in Korean women increases as more Western values permeate the social infrastructure of Korean society, according to the two findings. Kim et al.'s findings also differ from those of others – Results to the Contrary (RTC) – in that HB women in clinical samples held more traditional (non-Western) values. One's results either support or refute work already done; or each finding can do both throughout the course of a discussion section. Where relevant and appropriate, the codes RTC and RCL should be written in the right margin.

Throughout the first seven paragraphs of Kim et al.'s (2014) discussion, the authors repeat this process – ROF→RCL, ROF→RTC – always tying their primary findings to the larger literature, noting how their work supports or refutes the work that others have done. And, just as we saw in DiCataldo and Everett's (2008) discussion, Kim et al. are not finished. They must now critique their own article by pointing out the limitations of their work, as well as making recommendations for future research. Their first self-critique is that their sample was drawn from metropolitan areas where Western influence is prevalent; hence, they caution that their findings may not be generalizable to rural areas (Kim et al., 2014, p. 507). Finally, they point out that GAPs exist in the literature in the form of RFWs. Again, RFWs are made because the current state of the knowledge is necessarily incomplete. Consider the RFWs that Kim et al. proclaim:

(1) First, the IFR [Index of Family Relations Scale] used in our study measures the respondents' feelings about their family relationship as a whole, rather than their feelings about any specific relationships ... (3) Researchers should conduct future research to examine how women's feelings about different relationships with family members (e.g., husbands, in-laws, and children) might be related to HB symptoms. (4) Second, our finding of a significant relationship between profeminist gender beliefs and HB stimulates further questioning. (5) In particular, how are Korean women's egalitarian, feminist attitudes perceived in the family? Do family members support or accept the Korean women's perspective, and how does that contribute to more or fewer HB symptoms? (p. 507)

The preceding RFWs, which by default become GAPs, logically follow and emerge from the authors' current findings. That is, if current measures only reflect women's attitudes toward the family as a whole rather than specific relationships within the family, then it makes sense for future works to disentangle those measurement choices. Should any undergraduate student in health sciences, counseling, social work, or women's studies need ideas for an honors thesis or a senior-level capstone project; should any master's student in the aforementioned disciplines need a topic for his or her thesis; should a doctoral student need a topic to pursue as part of his or her PhD dissertation, all they need to do is find, and then use those RFWs as GAPs of their own. In other words, the potential new ideas for future works are buried in the text being read, again illustrating the importance of learning to read critically through the use of the reading codes. The first one to initiate and complete the project and publish the results gets dibs on the claims.

Eight paragraphs make up the discussion in Oliver and Armstrong's (1995) article on 'Predictors of viewing and enjoyment of reality-based and fictional crime shows,' published in *Journalism & Mass Communication Quarterly*. The first paragraph of the discussion begins the following way:

(1) The purpose of this study was to explore predictors of exposure to and enjoyment of reality-based crime programs. (2) Consistent with Zillmann's Disposition Theory, the results of this telephone survey suggest that these types of programs may be most appealing to viewers predicted to be particularly likely to enjoy the capture and punishment of criminal suspects who are often members of racial minorities. (3) Namely, this study found that reality-based programs were most enjoyed by viewers who evidenced higher levels of authoritarianism, reported greater punitiveness about crime, and reported higher levels of racial prejudice.

The first sentence repeats the main research question examined in the study; the code WTDD ought to be written in the right margin. The second sentence informs readers that the results of the study support the work of a previous researcher; hence, the code RCL ought to be written in the right margin. The third sentence provides the readers with the primary findings from the study: people who tend to be authoritarian, people who report greater punitiveness about crime, and those who tend to be racially prejudiced enjoy reality-based crime shows. The code ROF ought to be written in the right margin. The first paragraph is consistent with the form and structure of discussions that we have examined thus far: WTDD, ROF, RCL, RTC. Discussion sections are sites where the initial research question is repeated in the past tense, the primary results echoed, and then evaluated against the literature. Whether the reported results are consistent with the existing state of the knowledge or contradict it is played out in the discussion. Oliver and Armstrong (1995) do not explicitly tease out the social or policy implications of their work.

Simply noting if results support or contradict previous literature, as we have seen, is not enough. In the articles discussed thus far, the authors took time to bring to our attention the limitations and deficiencies that exist in their own works. For example, Oliver and Armstrong (1995, p. 565) write:

> While the present investigation did not attempt to directly assess the relative beneficial or harmful functions of reality-based programs, the idea that these shows appeal to viewers with punitive, authoritarian, and prejudiced attitudes is worthy of further investigation.

Put another way, the present study did not assess the benefits or harms of reality-based programs; however, that such shows appeal to those who tend to be conservative in their political orientation should be pursued further. This statement means that there is a GAP somewhere in the literature. Again, the authors do not simply end there. They specifically provide four Recommendations for Future Works (RFWs) that are based on the presence of GAPs in their own works (pp. 565–6): RFW #1 'future research may consider exploring reactions to these types of shows among a wider variety of respondents.' RFW #2: 'Further research may consider exploring the specific portrayals within this genre that appeal to viewers.' RFW #3: 'research could examine how long-term exposure may affect estimates of the prevalence of crime or the percentage of people of color who are involved in crime-related activities.' RFW #4: 'future studies may consider exploring how exposure to reality-based crime shows relates to perceptions and judgments about crimes witnessed or reported in other contexts.' Next to these sentences, the code RFW should be written in the right margin so that they are easily identifiable and retrievable. There are always GAPs in social science journal articles that could be used as POCs and serve as RATs in a future paper.

Nine paragraphs make up the discussion section of Hu and Ma's (2010) article on 'Mentoring and student persistence in college: A study of the Washington State Achievers Program,' published in *Innovative Higher Education*. The first paragraph begins in the following way:

> (1) This study showed that the assignment of college mentors varies by institutional types; (2) and public, four-year institutions seem to have done a better job in this regard. (3) Hispanic students and 'other' students are more likely than White students to seek support and encouragement from their mentors. (4) In addition, Hispanic students are more likely than their White counterparts to perceive their overall experiences with mentoring as more important. (5) Previous research has suggested that ethnic minority students report lower coping efficacy and expect to confront more educational and career-related barriers than White students [citation omitted].

(6) Thus, the findings of this study offer support for the hypothesis that mentoring experiences vary by race and ethnicity (Barker 2007; Nora and Crisp 2007). (p. 337)

The first four sentences repeat the ROFs of Hu and Ma's study. They do not repeat what they did in their study (WTDD); they simply inform the readers about the significant results of their study. These ROFs should be highlighted, and the code ROF written in the right margin. Notice how the ROFs in sentences #1–4 are interpreted against the broader literature in sentence #5. Sentence #5 provides the background or the previous literature (SPL) against which the current ROFs are interpreted, that minority students expect to face more difficulty than White students. It is this SPL that sentence #6 pushes against; it turns out that one of Hu and Ma's ROFs is consistent with (RCL) what Barker (2007) and Nora and Crisp (2007) have reported in prior works. The code RCL should be written in the right margin. Such interpretive moves are played out again in later paragraphs.

In the first paragraph, then, Hu and Ma (2010) do what scholars in other disciplines have done: repeat their main findings (ROFs) and interpret their findings relative to the work that others have done. Primarily, those interpretive possibilities exist in two forms: results that support previous research (RCL) or results that contradict established findings (RTC). It is this contextualization and interpretation of one's findings and arguments that are accomplished in discussion sections. Without such linkages to the broader literature, one's findings and arguments become orphans in a community of scholars and knowledge claims, unconnected to the genealogy of their ideas. There are times, however, when ROFs require a bit more extended discussion and elaboration, especially when unexpected results of a study are encountered. Consider the following fifth paragraph of Hu and Ma's (2010) discussion section:

(1) Considering that the frequency of contact has been identified as an important aspect of the student–mentor relationship [citation omitted] and that it is reported to be positively related to students' adjustment to college [citation omitted] and persistence [citation omitted], it is somewhat surprising to find that the number of meetings with college mentors is not significantly related to the probability of persisting by the WSA recipient in this study. (2) It is uncertain whether this result arises from the combination of the nature of the college mentoring programs affiliated with the WSA program and the distinct feature of the sample used in the study. (3) In addition, all the mentees in this study are high-achieving, low-income students. (4) They are different from the 'at-risk' mentees in many mentoring programs sponsored by individual institutions. (5) This should be taken into consideration in understanding the findings of this study. (p. 338)

In the first half of sentence #1, Hu and Ma (2010) reiterate findings from previous research (SPL); in the second half, they report their ROF and interpret it against the literature. The phrase 'it is somewhat surprising' suggests that their ROF is not consistent with the literature as well as their expectations. Therefore, the code RTC, Results to the Contrary, would be the most appropriate code to write in the right margin. Notice, however, that the unexpected nature of Hu and Ma's finding leads to speculation and further elaboration. They are almost compelled to explain this unexpected outcome and sentences #2–5 do exactly that: they qualify and offer educated conjectures about why the unexpected results may have been found: maybe the current sample was different from prior studies; the WSA sample was composed of high-achieving but low-income students: 'This should be taken into consideration in understanding the findings of this study' (p. 338). Hu and Ma (2010) are offering their readers ways to understand the unexpected findings of their work.

What Hu and Ma (2010) do not do is provide a roadmap of what is still missing in the literature and the work that future researchers ought to do. In other words, they do not make recommendations for future works (RFWs). That absence should not mean GAPs do not exist. The study that Hu and Ma conducted can be critiqued on some points (POC): they may have missed an obvious connection to a previous claim (MOP) or future scholars can cultivate a POC and pursue it further in their own paper (RPP). Discussion sections, whether in sociology, psychology, criminology, nursing, or education, generally end with RFWs due to the tentative state of the knowledge in the social sciences, and as a way of moving the literature forward. More work could always be done to improve the state of the literature. Consider how those RFWs occur in the discussion section of the article by Thapa, Cohen, Guffey, and Higgins-D'Alessandro (2013), published in *Review of Educational Research*:

(1) As this review makes clear, the majority of studies do not examine the effects of climate within multilevel/hierarchical frameworks, and very few examine school change over time, a key to understanding school improvement processes and efforts. (2) Building on the important school improvement research that Bryk and his colleagues (2002, 2010) have conducted in Chicago, we suggest that more studies examine school climate from multiple perspectives, including experimental, quasi-experimental, and correlational, as well as case studies and qualitative analyses, and as much as possible integrate process and outcome concepts into time-sensitive analyses. (p. 371)

The preceding paragraph is the second to the last paragraph of the entire article entitled 'A review of school climate research,' and in the article, the phrase 'we suggest that more studies examine ...' appears in the discussion section and would be aptly coded as an RFW, for that is what the authors are doing. Thapa et al. (2013) are suggesting that future scholars conduct the type of work that they recommend. Why would they make such a recommendation? After reviewing numerous previous studies in their article on school climate, they are pointing out the shortcomings that still exist in the literature on school climate. RFWs are shortcomings that exist in the literature, and should be treated as such: they should be faithfully written in the right margins when they are spotted.

How to Read the Conclusion Section

Robert Entman's (1990) article entitled 'Modern racism and the images of blacks in local television news,' published in *Critical Studies in Mass Communication*, examines how local news challenges conventional views of racism and facilitates it at the same time. There is no discussion section; three paragraphs, however, make up the conclusion section of the article. In the first paragraph, the author summarizes the ROFs from the current study: showing blacks as offenders and victims makes them look ominous, thereby perpetuating a negative stereotype, while showing positive images of blacks in the news leads to the false impression that racial discrimination is no longer a significant problem. In the second paragraph, Entman goes on to explain the paradox of news as it relates particularly to blacks. He states that the constraints and market-driven and standard operating practices of TV journalism, rather than malicious intention, may account for the paradoxical outcome that local news produces. He ends the second paragraph by stating that, 'The implication of this research, then, is that local news is likely to continue the practices hypothesized here' (p. 343). In the third and final paragraph, Entman (1990) writes the following:

(1) To be sure, images of blacks in the local news are complicated and replete with multiple potential meanings. (2) And audiences bring to the news a variety of predispositions. (3) Social scientists have no more than a rudimentary understanding of how audiences perceive and process media messages [citations omitted]. (4) Nonetheless, the exploratory study provides ample support for a hypothesis that local television's images of blacks feed racial anxiety and antagonism at least among that portion of the white population most predisposed to those feelings. (5) Quantitative research on the impact of exposure to local TV news seems in order, as does extensive content analysis of large samples of local and network news. (6) Such work would also illuminate the ways that television helps to alter and preserve dominant cultural values and structures of power. (p. 343)

The main thrust of the conclusion is that local news carries several meanings; as the last sentence suggests, TV – local news – shapes and maintains culture and power. The paradoxical way that local news creates and debunks racism is again reflected in a much broader context in the conclusion. Moreover, the author's work is consistent with his initial hypothesis. His work, however, is not complete. He proffers two RFWs: (1) additional quantitative research of exposure impact, and (2) more content analysis using larger samples of local and network news. The code RFW should be written in the right margin. Although no discussion section is present, readers can see that certain components are essential elements of the conclusion. The larger meaning of the current study is teased out; limitations of current research and recommendations for future works are stated in the conclusion, despite the absence of a discussion.

In the discussion and conclusion sections we have read through, we have seen how the authors have made their ROFs relevant and meaningful by linking their works with past research; furthermore, we have seen how the authors have teased out the policy implications of their work – doing in their papers what numerous how-to books have instructed students to do. That does not mean POCs do not exist. In fact, the authors themselves might have Missed an Obvious Point (MOP) and this MOP can be used as a POC to be RPPed in a future paper. MOP should be written in the right margin. For instance, one of the implications that Sampson (1987) teases out in his article is that black men face economic deprivation and labor-market marginality, which can then lead to family disruption and crime. One of the scholars that Sampson cited, William Wilson, argues that black men face and have faced structural impediments to employment by being segregated in inner cities, black men display characteristics that make them less attractive to potential employers, black men have been the first to lose their jobs in the deindustrialization that took place in rustbelt cities. That is, black men face cumulative disadvantage of sorts. So, if an astute reader asks why black men have faced economic deprivation and labor-market marginality, how might Sampson answer this question? To find a cogent and comprehensive answer, that reader will have to go outside of sociology and criminology; the answer to that question lies in disciplines such as history and communication. Even the most influential articles published in the highest-tier journals, written by a highly influential scholar teaching at one of the most prestigious institutions, can be critiqued; even such scholarship can be CPLed and used as a POC and RPP in a future paper. That process begins during the act of reading.

As argued throughout this book, the reading codes serve several purposes. First, they slow down the act of reading so that readers do not gloss over words and phrases; by enacting the role of a textual detective during the act of reading, readers are trying to figure out the function of a particular text in addition to processing its contents. Reading therefore occurs on two levels. Second, reading with codes leads to critical thinking during the act of reading. Rather than reflecting on the merits or limitations of an article after the reading is completed, the use of reading codes engages the reader with the text in real time, while the reading is taking place. Problems of recall and memory are thus minimized since observations and notes about the readings are made on the text itself. The use of reading codes structures the mind toward a purposive task with realizable objectives that can be accomplished, thereby avoiding unstructured – unproductive – reading. The use of reading codes leads to questions such as 'What function does this sentence/paragraph serve in the article?' rather than 'What did I just read for the last 15 minutes?'

By identifying sentences and paragraphs that perform a particular function (RCL, RTC, RPP, RFW, MOP) within a social science article, students are not only thinking critically and evaluating the paper's strengths and weaknesses, but they are also implicitly structuring their own papers to write in the future. That is, readers are identifying the relevance of current research to the past literature, and spotting deficiencies and gaps in the literature for their own exigent (e.g., end-of-semester literature review paper) and future-oriented tasks (e.g., thesis, dissertation). That is why reading cannot be treated as a secondary activity. Before a writer can even think about constructing an outline, the contents of that outline have to be filled in somehow. The left margin thematic codes along with the themes in the SPLs in the right margins proffer a starting point for an outline. As argued in this book, trying to recall the contents of 50-plus articles and trying to organize them in some cogent way are daunting tasks: the reading codes facilitate the organization and management of information necessary for academic writing.

6

Highlighting and Organizing the ROF, SPL, CPL, GAP, RFW, and POC

One of the notable mistakes I have seen again and again when I check students' primary reading materials (e.g., books, articles) is the highlighted blocks of text in various colors. That is, rather than using a highlighter to emphasize useful and important points (useful and important being defined as points that can be used toward easy retrieval and incorporation of pertinent information from the text into an ongoing writing project), students highlight entire paragraphs, sometimes even pages, falsely believing that entire paragraphs are sufficiently important to warrant their highlight. Simply put, students do not use highlighters appropriately. Highlighting entire paragraphs constitutes nothing short of highlighter abuse.

As I have attempted to demonstrate in previous chapters, and as notable composition teachers have pointed out (e.g., Strunk & White, 1979), pages and paragraphs are not organized in formless ways. The first sentences of paragraphs perform functions that differ from the rest of the sentences in them. First sentences introduce main ideas in a summarizing sort of way while the rest of the sentences that follow support them. I have argued in this book that readers can structure their reading so that the contents of social science journal articles can be anticipated and classified along predictable and recurring patterns. Once this internal structure and logic of social science journal articles is understood, the blocks of texts – paragraphs that coalesce into pages – should be seen for what they are: as one ring in a logical chain of paragraphs. The authors that you are reading are trying to persuade you to their line of argumentation. They want to convince you that what they are trying to say in the article makes sense; by the time an article appears in a peer-reviewed journal, the authors have persuaded two to three other academics that the paper has merit and ought to be published.

The Tools of Academic Reading

We have all done it on Sunday afternoons. We have, at one time or another, sat back on the velvet-draped couch, put our feet up on the coffee table or slung our legs over the armrest, held up the book (usually a mystery or a romance novel) in mid-air with one hand, and lazily thumbed through the pages. This scene is pleasure reading at its best. In university libraries across North America, I have witnessed students mimicking this posture on wooden chairs and desks – putting their feet up on desks and curling up in institutional chairs as they would do at home. This attempt to reproduce idyllic Sunday afternoon reading in a library is bad for one's back and the absolutely wrong way to read. Such a posture ought to be reserved for pleasure reading where students do not have to worry about summarizing and critiquing the state of the literature as well as finding ways to justify the rationale for their projects. Reading social science journal articles is a purposive task; and like other goal-oriented tasks, the right tools and the right techniques are essential components of the reading process. In fact, the two are inextricably intertwined.

Reading social science journal articles – if I may – does not bring a sense of joy that one receives from reading, let's say, the Book of Ecclesiastes, the Book of Psalms, Shakespeare, or Pushkin. Reading social science journal articles, for most professional social scientists, and graduate and undergraduate students in the social sciences, is work. And as such, it ought to be treated like work. That means reading academic texts ought to be approached differently from pleasure-related texts. The first step in correct reading entails assuming the right posture. Readers ought to sit at a desk of some sort, preferably with a hard surface, and mentally and physically prepare to read actively. Trying to read academic texts as one would read a romance novel – curled up on a sofa – is apt to lead to meandering reading. By assuming a correct – working – posture, we dignify reading as work rather than something leisurely; by conceptualizing and executing reading as a form of work, we do it irrespective of our personal preference and taste. We do it because it is a job, and it needs to be done. That is why writing problems that other scholars have noted are not attributable to motivation. That is, police officers, nurses, and janitors do not have to be particularly motivated to answer 911 calls, take care of patients, and clean toilets; they do it to pay bills and eat. If academics treated reading and writing like other working-class people treated their jobs, there would be no motivation problems and writers' blocks.

Second, as I have recommended in the preceding chapters, readers should engage with the text actively. Active reading is the opposite of meandering reading, just as pleasure reading is the corporeal opposite of academic reading. As argued earlier, marking reading codes during the act of reading facilitates cognitive boundary demarcation through a purposive task orientation – that is, reading with a concrete objective in mind and end in sight. This engagement was done actively in two ways: writing reading codes in the right margins and thematic codes in the left margins. Thus, rather than wrestling with the problem of memory and recall after the act of reading is completed, code insertions force readers to engage the text in real time during the act of reading, thus interrupting meandering trains of useless thoughts that creep in, by corporeally engaging the body and the mind during the act of reading.

I have found that three tools facilitate the reading process: (1) ruler, (2) pen, (3) highlighter (Figure 5).

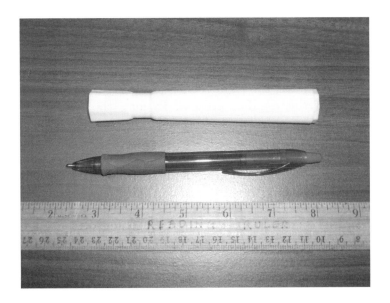

FIGURE 5

A ruler's primary function during the act of reading is to interrupt the series of jumps (saccades) our eyes make along a line by delineating the perceptual boundaries of texts (Rayner & Pollatsek, 1989). That is, rather than becoming overwhelmed by the number of pages in an article and lines on a page that have to be read, the ruler demarcates sentence boundaries in order to contain the task of reading to one sentence at a time. This way, readers are forced to slow down the act of reading to prevent mindlessly jumping from sentence to sentence horizontally and paragraph to paragraph vertically – becoming lost in meandering reading.

Second, by using a pen to write reading and thematic codes in the margins, readers again slow down the act of reading at the sentence and paragraph level by identifying the respective functions of sentences and themes in paragraphs. As I have argued in earlier chapters, directives to read 'critically,' although benign in intent, are useless without palpable instructions for students to follow. Marking reading codes during the act of reading constitutes a critical engagement with the text and the author, since readers are not passively imbibing the information contained therein; instead, the reader is summarizing, critiquing, and connecting the reading to the broader literature (e.g., RCL, RTC, MOP, POC); in that sense, marking reading codes during the act of reading constitutes a literal and dialogical performance of the 'critical' in critical reading. As one can see, it is nearly impossible to use a ruler and a pen during the act of reading in a pleasure-reading posture, nor can a student read passively when doing critical reading. The reading tools mentioned in this chapter are meant to assist in that critical reading process.

Third, highlighters are meant to emphasize – highlight – important points in a text. So how should student readers decide what is important and what to highlight? In the context of social science journal articles, that choice is constrained by the structure, logic, and form that are inherent in texts themselves. If students employ the Reading Code Organization Sheet (RCOS, see Figure 6), they should never have to wonder what to highlight. As shown in previous chapters, social science journal articles are organized in logical and predictable ways. The highlighter abuse problem occurs because novice students have not understood the form of the journal articles. Once the functions of SPL, CPL, GAP, RAT, ROF, and POC are understood, deciding what to highlight also should not occur indiscriminately or randomly. ROFs are the primary claims that authors of social science journal articles are trying to make; the ROFs will become the SPLs in the papers that students are trying to write – they are the most important components of a journal article when reading. They constitute the answers to the question 'What's the article about?' Therefore, the ROFs ought to be highlighted. GAPs are another important part of the writing process so they are also highlighter-worthy during the reading process. If a student uses one color to highlight all ROFs and another color to highlight GAPs throughout her literature review, the colors will make identification and retrieval much easier. Of course, another student may choose to use a different-colored highlighter for each reading code (e.g., red for all SPLs, blue for CPLs, etc.), but the rainbow of colors may lead to highlight overkill and create another type of highlighter abuse, thus vitiating its effectiveness.

Reading Code Management

In Chapter 4, we discussed how to construct a literature review. As part of crafting a literature review, it was noted that ROFs from the current literature will become the SPLs of the to-be-written paper. I also mentioned at length one of the cardinal sins of any literature review – the laundry list problem. To avoid that mistake, it was suggested summaries of previous literature be synthesized – organized thematically, whether the theme was methodological, conceptual, or analytical – not author by author, year by year. Moreover, in addition to a thematic summary of the previous literature, a critique of previous literature leading to a GAP also had to be incorporated in a competently executed literature review. Using the reading codes to organize, cultivate, and develop themes in summaries and critiques was described as 'making the quarter turn,' for using the way the literature has been organized in previous studies and mining them for existing patterns and trends is a technique to be exploited to justify one's own proposed study.

Although such a strategy appears to be questionable and problematic, it is consistent with the business and practice of academic publishing. Again, professional academics are in the business of wheel modification, not wheel reinvention. An undergraduate research paper, a capstone paper, or an honors thesis does not have to make contributions to the literature the way a master's thesis or a PhD dissertation does. They just have to be sufficiently original and creative to impress the student's instructors. A study, thesis, or dissertation does not have to be radically innovative; it just has to be sufficiently innovative to earn the affirmative votes of thesis and dissertation committee members. An article submitted to a journal to be considered for publication does not have to be paradigm-shifting work; it just has to be sufficiently innovative to earn the affirmative votes of reviewers. While the aforementioned attitude may appear to plant the seeds of mediocrity, undergraduate students who have looming graduation deadlines and graduate students who have to worry about the expiration of their funding do not have the luxury of working on a dissertation or paper until it is capable of shifting paradigms. Those days of luxury – working on a single paper or a book for years on end that radically shifts paradigms – if they ever existed, are long gone in academia.

To mine for patterns and themes to organize one's literature review, I recommended going through each article and identifying all SPLs, CPLs, GAPs, POCs, and RFWs by perusing through the left and right margins. By going through the SPLs and CPLs, themes and patterns in the way the literature and its critiques are organized can be used as reference points to organize one's own literature review. For small projects such as an original research paper for a capstone course, or an undergraduate honors thesis, looking through each and every article collected for the literature review is a manageable task. For literature reviews and papers that require more than 40 articles, inspecting each and every article for patterns in the way previous SPLs and CPLs are organized is a daunting task, especially if one has to carry around the articles. This burden means that a much more centralized method of organizing the information gathered from the readings is necessary.

Article #	Author, year	ROF	SPL	CPL	GAP	RFW	POC/RPP
1							
2							
3							
4							
5							
6							
7							
8							
9							
100							

FIGURE 6   Reading Code Organization Sheet (RCOS)

The Reading Code Organization Sheet (RCOS) (Figure 6) is meant to facilitate the identification and retrieval of requisite information gathered from the readings in order to cultivate a synthesis of the literature. Rather than looking through each and every article, page by page, the seven reading codes that are essential to constructing a literature review should serve as the starting point for academic writing for students. Obviously, an RCOS will only be as useful as the information that is put into it, but, assuming that there is correct input, the output should be more manageable than the traditional methods used (e.g., index cards, memory, intuition). Ideally, students should enter reading codes into RCOS on the day the articles are read. So, for example, if a student has set aside one day of the week for reading/writing and has used that day to read six journal articles, she should enter the reading code summaries into the RCOS upon their completion. Realistically, for whatever reason, students may not be able to complete the RCOS immediately upon completion of the readings. Should the same student return to her task a day or two later, after the exigencies of life have passed, she should not have to look through the articles to find out what their main claims are, what their shortcomings and critiques are, and what recommendations for future works the authors have made because those important points will have been noted in the margins and highlighted. All that remains to be done is the mechanical act of entering the summaries of codes into the RCOS. Such activities would count as prewriting. For example, a sample sheet might look like Figure 7.

Since the publication of the first edition of *How to Read Journal Articles in the Social Sciences*, several classes have used the reading codes to organize their notes and papers. Consequently, a much more accurate assessment of the workload involved in using an RCOS, such as the one in Figure 7, can be provided. According to students, a 15–20-page journal article takes about 1.5 to 2 hours to read, inserting the reading codes where relevant. They also report that inserting codes for one journal article into an RCOS takes about 10–20 minutes. For a minimum of 30 sources that are used in a research paper, students can expect to spend about 70-plus hours reading and entering data into an RCOS. Of course, the obsessive and compulsive students – the overachieving nerds – manage to read about 40–45 articles for their papers so their workload is substantially increased. Students who are accustomed to using 5–7 references for a paper are shocked at the back-breaking amount of work that writing an original research paper in the last year of their undergraduate education entails.

Students also report that completing an RCOS is an exercise in medieval torture: they state that they often wished that I (PS) would die a painful death or experience some other physical misfortune in life for the pain and misery that an RCOS – or to be more precise, I – caused them, for forcing them to read journal articles using the reading codes and organizing their notes using an RCOS. I am quite certain that students entertained homicidal fantasies as a compensatory mechanism to alleviate their feelings of powerlessness.

Article #	Author, year	ROF	SPL	CPL	GAP	RFW	POC/RPP
1	DiCataldo & Everett (2008)	1. Non-killers had higher delinquency rating than killers 2. Situational forces (guns, alcohol) may explain outcome rather than psychopathological personality	1. Extensive interest 2. Definition 3. Cause 4. Method 5. Mental health 6. Substance abuse 7. Gun availability 8. Stereotype	1. Scientific validity of term 2. No control group 3. Questionable sample 4. No theory integration	1. Scientific validity of term 2. No control group 3. Questionable sample 4. No theory integration	1. Differential processing 2. Explore motivation and circumstances 3. Explore offense characteristics + offender characteristics	1. 67.9% of adol. non-killers had anger problems while 37.5% of adol. killers reported anger problems

FIGURE 7   RCOS sample entry

(Some students have even proudly admitted such violent fantasies when prod-ded.) What became evident once I met with the students one-on-one after their RCOS completion was the level of confidence that they exuded. Students were able to summarize the literature, and identify recurring themes and potential shortcomings in the literature. As they did so, their competence and confi-dence became evident in suprasegmental ways: students' voices increased in volume; the speed of their delivery increased; their pitch intensified. They also smiled and became visibly excited when describing the state of the literature. That type of experience is aptly described as the joy of reading. In those moments, I was – am – proud to be a teacher, for I had helped my students become budding scholars in their own right.

I would be lying, however, if I were to proclaim that having students use the reading codes and RCOS for their papers (final papers, theses) resulted only in greeting card moments. It did not. The task of writing a research paper where students were required to produce an original claim/argument was debilitating for some. The sheer amount of work involved in reading and note-taking (prewriting), in addition to the actual writing process, caused some students quite a bit of anxiety; some students just stopped coming to class. Some students tried to falsify their RCOS entries, conjuring up the-matic codes and GAPs out of thin air. Students who attempted to misrepresent their work were always caught, for they were not able to answer simple ques-tions they should have known. Those students are caught because they have not read the literature and are trying to extemporaneously come up with the correct – plausible – answers. This type of deception produces stress and cues that become perceptible to experienced observers. When given the chance to confess their 'crimes,' they usually do. Students should understand that the requirements for their papers and the deadlines for their completion do not go away. It is simply easier to do the work honestly rather than through some duplicitous means. Honest work is psychologically easier than having one's lie exposed in a one-on-one meeting with a professor who knows the litera-ture on the topic that the student has selected, and then experiencing the shame (not embarrassment) that follows when confronted with the obvious deception.

If a student searches the term 'juvenile homicide' in an academic search engine, the article by DiCataldo and Everett (2008) will result in a 'hit.' In fact, one may get an unmanageable number of hits. Again, suppose that our hypothetical student who is writing a research paper, an honors thesis, or a master's thesis on juvenile homicide whittles down the number of relevant articles she has to read to 60. The fundamental problem I have raised and attempted to answer is how to manage the volume of information that she will gather from reading those 60 articles. Now, suppose that our hypotheti-cal student entered the summaries of codes for the remaining 59 articles in an RCOS. Undoubtedly, she will see common themes that emerge in the SPL category; that is because, in order to discuss the works of previous research- ers in the field, the 59 authors she will have read will also have read the same influential works (e.g., Bender, Russell, Busch, Corder, Cornell, Duncan, Ewing, Heide, Lewis, Zagar). That is why there's bound to be convergence in literature reviews. Moreover, if the ROFs from 59 other articles are exam- ined, there's bound to be convergence as well. The ROFs from the 60 articles become part of the SPL in the literature review component of the research paper or thesis that our hypothetical student is writing. Taking those 60 articles, identifying recurring patterns and themes, and condensing them into 8–10 coherently and logically connected themes is what consti- tutes a synthesis of the literature.

Notice again that if there was a collection of 60 CPLs and GAPs, a pattern will emerge. Those recurring GAPs ought to serve as the genesis of a the- matically organized CPL that follows the SPL. In addition to GAPs, the said student can mine through RFWs; these can serve as CPLs of her own. RFWs exist because previous scholars have not examined that aspect of the topic. For example, that DiCataldo and Everett (2008) did not examine offense characteristics of juvenile homicides and circumstances surrounding the kill- ing can serve as GAPs in the literature that warrant remedy. If our hypothetical student wanted to examine the motivation and circumstances behind juvenile killings, that there is a GAP in this component of the litera- ture can function as a RAT behind why her master's thesis or a research paper is warranted.

Creating an Outline for a Literature Review

Once the recurring themes in SPLs and CPLs/GAPs are identified, the next step in the transition process from reading to writing is transferring those themes into an outline. Silvia (2007) notes outlining should not be considered as a prelude to actual – real – writing. He observes that writers who experi- ence trouble writing are the ones who do not form outlines: 'After trying to write blindly, they feel frustrated and complain about how hard it is to gener- ate words' (p. 79). He advises writers to 'get thoughts in order' before trying to write. If we ask how the contents of those thoughts and outlines are to be filled in, we would be right back at where we started. Others have not shown how to make the transition from reading to outlining to writing in a method- ical and operationally actionable way. Again, the reading codes are designed to facilitate the outlining and writing process.

In most academic writing that involves original research that entails data collection – an honors/senior thesis, a master's thesis, PhD dissertation, peer-reviewed journal article – the structure and format of those academic texts are essentially the same:

Introduction: SPL, CPL, RAT, WTD

Literature Review: SPL, CPL, GAP

Data and Methods: Description of data and plan of analysis

Results: ROF

Discussion and Conclusion: WTDD, ROF, RCL, RTC, RFW

One of the most time-consuming parts of academic writing is reading through the voluminous literature on a given topic. That difficulty is compounded by the fact that not only must a student writer summarize the current state of knowledge but she also must find a way to critique it, identify shortcomings in it, and improve upon it so that she can set up a rationale for why her own proposed work is necessary. Others who have written how-to books have instructed authors to 'describe relevant theories, review past research, and discuss in more detail the question that motivated' the research (Silvia, 2007, p. 82). While correct, such instructions fail to spell out how to describe, review, and discuss the voluminous state of the literature. Furthermore, such advice neglects to instruct writers how to critique previous research as a way of remedying knowledge gaps in the literature (see Harris, 2014). As I have argued, a more principled and methodical way of organizing and outlining a literature review before the actual writing begins is necessary.

By looking through a RCOS, a student should identify eight to ten (or how-ever many the paper requires) themes that can be used to summarize the literature. Usually, the ROFs and SPLs can be collapsed into one category to come up with eight to ten themes in most journal article-length papers. Students should use two sources as part of their literature review. First, once students look through the SPL column, they will see that certain thematic codes appear with regularity and frequency. Then, they must look through the ROF column and see that certain ROFs are similar to some SPL catego-ries. Students should be able to combine the SPL and ROF columns to create their own SPLs in their literature reviews: the ROFs that you have read become the SPLs of your paper. Then, one must find GAPs in the literature. Those GAPs and CPLs should be organized into three to five themes. Once those GAPs are identified, a student must then demonstrate how her research will overcome those deficiencies in the literature. This justification consti-tutes the RAT. The RAT should also be organized along three to five themes, and these RATs should be placed in the introduction. In outline form, a hypo-thetical literature review may look like the example on the following page.

In outline form, the task of reviewing the literature on a topic looks logical, simple, and rather easy to do. Without an outline, the voluminous state of a literature looks intimidating, amorphous, and difficult to navigate. To fill in themes one to eight, the student simply looks at the ROF and SPL columns and identifies those themes. She then elaborates on those themes at the paragraph level when writing. The topic sentence introduces and summarizes the topic to be covered in the paragraph; sentences that follow proffer support. By using themes to discuss the previous and current state of the literature, the laundry list problem and the practice of citing one author to death throughout the course of a paragraph (the 'beating one horse to death' problem) is avoided. If hypotheses are introduced, they would have to follow SPL and CPL/GAP. Whether one is setting up a RAT for a study or testing a hypothesis, both emerge naturally, logically, and expectably from the way the literature is synthesized and critiqued. It is the job of the author – you the student – to persuade the reader to 'see' that line of reasoning. By the time a reader finishes the literature review section there should be little doubt as to why the study that is being done is being done. That justification needs to begin from the first paragraph of the literature review and end before the last paragraph of that section.

Outline of a literature review

I. SPL

  A. Theme 1
  B. Theme 2
  C. Theme 3
  D. Theme 4
  E. Theme 5
  F. Theme 6
  G. Theme 7
  H. Theme 8

II. CPL/GAP

  A. GAP 1
  B. GAP 2
  C. GAP 3

Putting It All Together: Writing a Professional-quality Paper

One of the most intolerable ambiguities, not just in writing but also in life, is the absence of boundaries and constraints. For instance, imagine that you are given a backpack and instructed to march forward. You are not told how far you must march; you are not told if you can stop and take breaks; you are not told the pace at which you should march; you are not told when your march will end. You are not told the destination. Similarly, imagine that your professor tells you to write a paper. She does not tell you what the topic ought to be; she does not tell you the paper's acceptable length; she does not tell you which citation style to use; she does not tell you how many references you need in your paper. She does not even tell you when the paper is due. Some might say that both conditions represent absolute freedom – freedom to do whatever the hiker or the student author wants: unbridled room for creativity.

However, like most things in life, the notion of freedom (and academic writing) does not exist in such indeterminate states. Although we Westerners like to think that we exercise 'free speech,' we do not (Fish, 1994). We are constrained by what we cannot say legally, socially, and morally. That is, we can't walk up to a police officer and utter, 'I'm going to kill you!' and expect to receive first amendment protection when arrested for making terroristic threats; nor can we yell out 'Fire!' in a crowded theater and claim free speech. Furthermore, we can't say whatever harmful, hurtful, and deceitful things we want about others without legal repercussions (e.g., libel); and if we uttered whatever honest thought that came to mind in our interpersonal interactions, we would lead a very lonely and solitary existence very, very quickly. As Stanley Fish would say, 'there is no such thing as free speech and it's a good thing.' But despite such constraints that are placed on what we can say and write, notice that such restrictions do not place limits on what we can accomplish with language. Creative expressions of comedy, wit, irony, and tragedy abound in written and spoken forms of language despite restrictions and constraints.

The same types of boundaries and constraints exist in academic writing. Academic writing in its most revered and valued form – the peer-reviewed journal article – suffers from an even greater constraint than other forms of writing (e.g., novels, books) for one simple reason: space. Most journals have a finite amount of space available in each issue; if you sent a 20,000-word essay to most social science journals, my guess is that it would promptly be returned. Most social science journals have word limits on manuscript submissions. Such restrictions are both positive and negative. Such a restriction is good since it provides boundaries – authors know they can't exceed a certain word count and page limit; it is bad in the sense that it limits what authors are able to do in an article. At the extreme end, some journals are willing to accept a paper that is up to 15,000 words in length; most social science journals expect between 8,000 and 10,000 words in a single paper submission. For the purpose of illustration, I will use the lower word count. This limitation means that in 8,000 words, the following components have to be covered:

1. Cover page; title, name, affiliation
2. Abstract
3. Introduction
4. Literature Review
5. Data and Methods: Description of data and plan of analysis
6. Results
7. Discussion and Conclusion
8. References

Some student readers may be wondering what 8,000 words translates into; they need to comprehend that word count in the context of countable pages.

One single-spaced page of text in 12-point Times New Roman font will yield approximately 600 words; about 15–17 reference materials (books, book chapters, and articles) will fit into one single-spaced page of references, yielding about 300 words; dividing 8,000 by 600 results in 13.3 or about 14 single-spaced pages. Authors have 14 single-spaced pages to introduce the article, do a literature review, describe data and methods, display results, and discuss the results and implications of their findings relative to those of others in the field – plus the reference section. If you look at it from that perspective, 14 single-spaced pages or 8,000 words is not all that much. In fact, first-time writers may want additional space. Such greed is not practical, for journals are generally bound and restricted in their resources. It is therefore incumbent upon authors to exercise creativity and innovation within an already existing set of restrictions and constraints – like 'free' speech; and like 'free' speech the possibilities are endless.

The task before us now is how to allocate the 14 single-spaced pages to the eight sections of the 8,000-word paper. I have found that the task becomes more manageable if the reading codes are used to organize, identify, and fill in the contents of the sections (Table 6.1).

TABLE 6.1   Typical social science journal article format

Section	Textual function in article	Page amount (in single space)
Cover page	Paper title, name, affiliation	–
Abstract	SPL, CPL, ROF, WTD	0.5
Introduction	SPL, CPL, RAT, WTD	1
Literature Review	SPL, CPL, GAP	4–5
Data and Methods	Description of data and method of analysis	1.5–2
Results	ROF	1–2
Discussion and Conclusion	WTDD, ROF, RCL, RTC, RFW	2–3
References		3–5
Goal		14

Throughout this book, we have used sample social science articles as data to identify how they are structurally and textually organized. Abstracts tended to fall between 150 and 200 words; they were miniature reproductions of introductions in 150–200 words or less. If students need to write an abstract of their own, they should write sentences that resemble SPL, CPL, ROF, and WTD in 150 words or less. Introductions were composed of two to four paragraphs, generally not more than one single-spaced page that covered the SPL, CPL, and WTD. If students need to write an introduction for a paper that they are writing and thinking of sending to a journal, the students should write sentences that resemble SPL, CPL, and WTD in two to four paragraphs. Literature reviews and psychology introductions varied, but most would fall within a four to five single-spaced page range. Data and methods sections generally can be described in one to two pages; results, one to two; and discussion and conclusion, two to three.

Rather than blindly reading social science journals for simple content, this book has made the articles themselves the objects of analysis. That is, I attempted to identify what functions the sentences in abstracts, introductions, literature reviews, data and methods, and results and discussions and conclusions perform. By doing so, it was intended to organize the information contained in the readings in such a way as to make the writing process more manageable. Furthermore, by breaking down the constitutive elements of a social science journal article, I have tried to show how undergraduate and graduate students can undertake the task of writing an 8,000-word paper – should they be inclined and motivated to do so. The format provided above is one place to start. Emulating the authors that students have read by following a textual function approach delineated by paragraphs and pages is one way to go about accomplishing that task.

What students should not wonder about is how to fill in the contents of an outline and the article itself. As I have shown here, social science journal articles are organized in logical and predictable ways. By employing the reading codes, students should be able to write an article or an article-length paper on their own. As I have argued in this book, the literature review is one of the most central components of an article. As shown here, introductions are small-scale reproductions of literature reviews executed in two to four paragraphs. Literature reviews are made up of a thematic synthesis of previous works (SPL), and their critique (CPL, GAP) in four to five single-spaced pages. One organizes a literature review by looking through the RCOS and mining for commonly recurring themes. Data and methods and results sections are fairly straightforward, as the student author describes the data and how they were analyzed, and presents the results of findings. When writing up the discussion and conclusion, one must interpret those results in the context of the findings from previous works (i.e., RCL, RTC). As shown above, all of those elements occur within an already existing set of confined space and words.

Out of the several components of a journal article, the literature review exerts the greatest amount of ecological force on the structural and textual organization of academic writing. The literature review also takes up the greatest amount of space in journal articles. That is why a competently done literature review is important. And to do a competent literature review, students must read the work of other scholars. Students are unable to write not because they have not formed outlines, but because they haven't read enough relevant literature to be able to even form a coherent idea of an outline. Trying to write a paper without sufficient reading is like trying to speak a foreign language without having learned enough vocabulary. One may know the syntactic structure and grammatical rules of a language, but without adequate vocabulary to apply those rules, one is unlikely to produce meaningful utterances. In order to even think about writing an academic paper, one must read sufficiently; to write an academic paper of professional quality, one must read critically and translate those critiques into a cogent rationale for why that paper is necessary. Then one can collect the data, analyze the results, and write them up.

When reading journal articles, the ROFs constitute the primary nuggets of information that are important. As shown in earlier chapters, those ROFs will become the SPLs of the paper that a student is trying to write. When writing one's own paper, however, the literature review is the most crucial component of the journal article-writing process since it affects the backward (abstract, introduction) and forward (discussion, conclusion, reference) elements of a paper. Believe it or not, when academics are asked to review a paper for a journal, one of the first things that we read is neither the abstract nor the introduction – it is the references section. By reading through an author's references list, we can discern if the author has read enough and read the right stuff. Moreover, we can anticipate the logic of the argument to unfold in the paper to be reviewed.

By employing the reading codes during the act of reading, and entering the summaries of reading codes into the RCOS upon the completion of reading, the idea of how and what to write in a paper ought to emerge on its own. Once students read enough literature, read actively, and organize their readings into the sheet, the outline for an 8,000-word paper will almost emerge on its own and organize itself. If students are contemplating writing a professional-quality paper to submit to a journal, they should also consider another potential writing project that is considerably less intensive and demanding than the 8,000-word paper.

The Structure of Short Reports, Flash Reports, and Research Notes

In most of the social scientific disciplines, there are articles that are shorter than the average length of 8,000–10,000 words. In sociology and criminology, these are called 'research notes,' which run from 12 to 20 printed pages. In psychology, shorter-than-average papers come in two forms, 'short reports' and 'flash reports.' Short reports are research articles that are less than 5,000 words, flash reports less than 2,500 words. Despite their diminutive size, the work done in the three types of paper is essentially similar to the full-length articles we have seen thus far.

For instance, Usoof-Thowfeek, Janoff-Bulman, and Tavernini (2011, p. 1) carried out three studies to examine the role of 'automatic and controlled processes in moral judgments.' The article is six pages in print, much shorter than the 20–30 print pages of average journal articles. The article, consistent with the practice in psychology, places the literature review upfront and, in it, the authors summarize previous works (SPL) in a succinct three paragraphs before the following sentences appear in the fourth paragraph:

> (1) Haidt (2001, 2007) notes that moral 'reasoning' often functions as a post hoc process that provides evidence to support our automatic reactions, but he also recognizes that rational deliberation can alter our intuitive responses. (2) To date, however, few empirical studies have explored the relationship between automatic and controlled processing in moral judgments. (p. 1)

Again, notice that the disjunction marker provides a hint of the CPL/GAP to come in the second sentence. If three prior paragraphs have summarized the current state of the literature, the second sentence critiques it by pointing to a shortcoming within it. In the very next paragraph, the authors provide the rationale for the study: 'We believe that social harm may be a particularly important variable in understanding the relationship between automatic and controlled processes in the case of moral judgments' (p. 2). Following this rationale, the authors go on to introduce three hypotheses they are testing in the study. The rest of the report follows a format recognizably similar: a data and methods section that describes the materials, participants, and procedures used in the study, followed by a short results and discussion section particular to the first experiment. These processes are repeated for experiments 2 and 3. A general discussion is proffered at the end of the paper that interprets their ROFs in relation to prior work.

In Cao, Adams, and Jensen's (1997, p. 368) research note, the authors ask and resolve one question: 'The research reported in this article tests their [Wolfgang & Ferracuti, 1967] black subculture of violence thesis.' Before they can do so, however, they must first introduce what the subculture of violence thesis is, and critique it before they can claim the WTD. In this research note, published in *Criminology*, the literature review and introduction sections are collapsed into one section, similar to a psychology publication, and, in it, the authors discuss the work of Wolfgang and Ferracuti (SPL), before systematically stating the following points:

> The association between the subculture of violence among blacks and violent behavior remains largely inconclusive. (p. 368)

While Dixon and Lizotte directly measured individuals' beliefs in practice, they did not control for all of the independent variables proposed by Wolfgang and Ferracuti, such as employment and violent history. (p. 369)

Thus, existing studies on the subculture of violence indicate that race has been seriously neglected in direct tests and that beliefs in violence among southerners have received attention. (p. 369)

Based on the preceding CPLs and identified GAPs, the authors answer the 'So what?' question by explicitly stating how their work will remedy the existing shortcoming in the subculture of violence literature. One can readily see how the short reports are similar to and different from their full-length siblings. They are similar in that the structure of ideas begins with a summary of previous literature, then moves to a critique and a gap, which is then remedied. They are also different in that the topic addressed is very narrow, which constrains the literature to be reviewed into substantially fewer themes (and pages). This compression also reduces the ROFs derived, and their interpretation proffered relative to previous findings in the discussion section. If general introductions are sort of small-scale rehearsals of literature reviews, then we can understand research notes and short reports as smaller-scale versions of full-length research articles, for the work done in them is less, but their form and structure are similar.

Once students are motivated enough to write and complete an article or a research note, it should definitely be reviewed by a faculty advisor before they send it to a journal; and before a journal is considered as a potential outlet for full-length papers or research notes, undergraduate and graduate students should consider another outlet – student paper competitions sponsored by their respective disciplines. In some cases, the top prize paper is published in a journal if the disciplinary association is the one that organized and sponsored the competition, and the standards of judgment are likely to be less stringent than professional reviews. Student paper competitions are good places to get one's feet wet before jumping into a pool with shark-like reviewers.

7

Will the Reading Code Organization Sheet Work on Non-social Science Texts?

I have thus far argued that the act of reading precedes the act of writing for the simple reason that before a student can begin to write, before she can even begin to put together an outline to think about writing, she must have an idea of what to write. In the context of social scientific writing (i.e., a research paper), the 'what to write' is shaped by the rationale that justifies the paper's existence. I argued that this rationale emerges from a thematically organized summary of existing literature as well as a cogently argued critique which identifies some gap in it. Simply put, for most research-oriented social scientific writing, authors must be able to answer the 'So what?' question. And to be able to provide a sufficient answer to that brutally simple question, a deficiency that exists in the knowledge has to be remedied in the proposed work. In a research paper that examines a substantive issue, topic, or problem – whether it is a research paper for a capstone course, an honors thesis, a master's thesis, a PhD dissertation, or a journal article – the author must be able to convince readers why that proposed piece of scholarship is necessary.

Using the social science journal article as a model, I have attempted to show that the structures of text in those articles are predictably organized. I demonstrated that those blocks of text perform a very particular textual function in social science articles. One of the most ecological components of a research paper, I argued, was the literature review, as it affected the forward and backward elements of any research paper. Throughout Chapters 3, 4, and 5, I instructed students on how to read various elements of a journal article (e.g., abstract, introduction, literature review). In Chapter 6, I provided simple ways of managing the information gathered from the reading codes using an organization sheet as a way of engaging in the prewriting process – thematically organizing the previous literature and results of findings from journal articles – before doing the actual writing. I also introduced the notion of constraint as a necessary and practical ethic for those writing professional-quality papers.

We have used social science journal articles from disciplines such as criminology, psychology, sociology, education, health, and communication to demonstrate the applicability and practical utility of the reading codes. In this chapter, I want to see if the reading codes might be applicable to other non-social science disciplines, disciplines that are more theoretical (i.e., absence of empirical data) and abstract (e.g., philosophy). By doing so, I hope to show readers that scholarly work in general is organized along the lines I have described and not just the social sciences. It is my contention that findings from research or arguments that are made in the context of academic scholarship in general always exist in relation to an already existing claim, that ideas, whether in the social sciences or humanities, exist in a dialectical fashion.

The first article that will be examined was published in the *American Political Science Review* entitled 'Church and state in Stanley Fish's antiliberalism,' written by J. Judd Owen (1999). Although the article selected for scrutiny does not 'count' as one of the disciplines in the humanities, the topic of liberalism is usually discussed in political philosophy. In the context of political science, political theory is considered a subfield of the American Political Science Association, the main governing body of the discipline. While most of the research that is carried out in political science is empirical, data-driven, quantitative, and falls under the purview of social sciences, political theory is one area where the relevant theorists, writing style, and modes of argumentation bear a much stronger resemblance to philosophy than other social sciences. For such reasons, Owen's article was selected.

In Owen's (1999, p. 911) article there are exactly 100 words in the abstract. The four sentences that make up the abstract do very similar work to the ones we have examined thus far.

(1) Even though they contain one of the most forceful critiques of liberalism in contemporary political thought, the political writings of Stanley Fish have been neglected by political theorists. (2) Fish's critique of liberal claims of moral and religious neutrality points to the conclusion that the liberal separation of church and state lacks a coherent justification. (3) I offer a qualified defense of liberalism by arguing that while Fish's critique of liberal neutrality is sound, he fails to do justice to liberalism's substantive basis. (4) Moreover, by simply negating liberalism, Fish's thinking remains within the liberal horizon in a way he fails to recognize.

The first sentence does the work of critiquing previous literature (CPL) and pointing out a GAP in existing literature. Simply put, Owen states that although the writings of Stanley Fish contain ideas that are relevant for political theorists, they have been neglected as objects of inquiry. Political theorists have not closely examined the implications of Fish's works for their discipline. The word 'neglect' hints that something is missing in the current state of the literature. The second sentence summarizes the work of one theorist; in fact, the writings of Stanley Fish are one of the main topics to be covered in the paper. Hence, as background material, sentence #2 counts as an SPL. The third sentence does the work of a WTD, for in it the author tells readers what he will do in the paper ('qualified defense of liberalism'), as well as point out another CPL in previous work ('he fails to do justice to liberalism'). Thus, in exactly 100 words, the abstract in Owen's article does work that is similar to the ones we have examined thus far in social science journal articles. The abstract provides a brief summary of the literature, a critique of it, and what the author will do to remedy the deficiency in the literature.

Owen's (1999) article is also structurally organized in a recognizably similar form to the ones we have examined thus far. The paper is organized into five major sections, with headings that sufficiently describe the topic covered in that major section. In those five sections, the author discusses the work of previous researchers, critiques them, and identifies a GAP in their works which he proposes to remedy. This step is rehearsed first in the abstract and then in the two paragraphs that precede the first major section, and comprise what could aptly be called an 'introduction.' In the first paragraph of the introduction, Owen goes on to summarize the aspects of Stanley Fish's works that are pertinent for political theory (SPL); then toward the end of the second paragraph, the following sentences appear:

> (1) Fish is an influential proponent of antifoundationalism, which maintains that all claims to knowledge are made from a particular and partisan perspective, are 'socially constructed', and therefore are never impartial or objective. (2) Radical as this doctrine is in itself, the singular radicalness of Fish's critique is the result of his focus on a potentially explosive area that seems to have escaped the notice of many political theorists: the theoretical juncture between antifoundationalism and the liberal doctrines concerning religion, which are the basis of liberal constitutionalism. (3) ... (4) This essay lays out Fish's critique and offers a limited defense against it. (Owen, 1999, p. 911).

Similar to the sentences that precede it, sentence #1 summarizes the main ideas of a previous scholar (Stanley Fish). In sentence #2, however, the phrase 'seems to have escaped' provides a clue that there might be something missing in the current state of the literature. So what is that missing element in the research? An examination of the 'theoretical junction between antifoundationalism and liberal doctrines concerning religion.' That is, no one has examined how antifoundationalism as a school of thought might affect the intersection of liberalism and religion – 'a potentially explosive area.' Such an assertion constitutes a GAP in the literature and, one sentence later, Owen tells readers how he will remedy that gap: lay out Fish's critique of liberalism (SPL) and offer a defense of liberalism (WTD). Readers can anticipate and expect that the rest of the article will do just that: offer a summary (SPL) of Fish's main ideas (Fish's critique of liberalism) before critiquing Fish's critique (CPL/GAP); then he will go on to defend the very thing that Fish has critiqued.

Sentence #4 constitutes a WTD, for the author tells readers what he will do in his paper. But notice what is missing: there is no sentence that can stand as an explicit RAT as we have seen in other social science articles. Readers are left to infer the necessity of the proposed work – rationale – by pointing out a GAP. One might call this practice 'reading between the lines,' for logically, the RAT lies between a GAP and a WTD. We might thus speculate that one unique feature of humanities texts might be that the reader is expected to do a bit more work; that extra work entails the activity of inferring. Given proposition A, then conclusion C, the process of inferring B that is unspoken is left to the reader – the paradigmatic structure of syllogistic reasoning. Unless one is explicitly taught this logical structure of arguments, or is sufficiently motivated to investigate this pattern, readers are apt to miss that hidden step in the reading process. We might tentatively state that this step is one way that social science articles differ from philosophical texts. Social science articles leave little room for reader inference. The various elements of the reading codes – as signs of textual work being done in the text – appear again and again throughout a paper.

Notice also the triadic character of the scholarship process that binds social sciences and humanities. Fish's critique of liberalism constitutes previous literature, a pre-existing body of ideas, and a summary of results of findings (in a social scientific sense) from previous works; in essence then, Fish's critique of liberalism is Owen's SPL. Owen describes previous works – the first major section entitled 'religion and the demise of liberal rationalism' – as 'sinuous.' That word does a lot of work, for it traces the genealogical indebtedness of contemporary political and legal theory to philosophers such as Thomas Hobbes, René Descartes, Immanuel Kant, Friedrich Nietzsche, John Stuart Mill, and John Rawls. Those names are practically a who's who of Western intellectual history, and to say that their ideas are 'interesting' would be a gross understatement. 'Sinuous,' however, eloquently and succinctly captures the winding, curving, and meandering course of Western political philosophy in the past 500 years. That is to say, before one can understand Fish's critique of liberalism, one must at least have some background knowledge of what is liberalism.

The problem that political theorists have struggled to bracket is differences in moral and philosophical views that lead to conflict between individuals and states. One can see why fundamental differences in moral, philosophical, and political views might be fraught with potential conflict. Differences and disagreements about notions of right and wrong, and about which god to worship and its methods of worship have led – continue to lead – to conflicts between nations and individuals – 'a potentially explosive area.' Liberalism's objective since its inception has been to devise a way to create a stable political order in societies by focusing on how public goods (e.g., jobs, benefits) are distributed fairly (i.e., procedures, methods) rather than defining the constitutive features of that public good (content), precisely so that individual differences in religion, morality, and tastes do not affect political institutions. Fish's critique of liberalism is that once a person sets aside his or her most cherished beliefs and values (e.g., religious doctrines), those beliefs no longer can be claimed to be what they are: core values that constitute the religion that believers profess them to be. Fish's critique of liberalism is that it might as well be another form of the church (that is, not content-less), despite its claim to be neutral and procedural; his critique is that liberalism is incoherent and confused. So what is Owen's critique of Fish's previous work? 'The ramifications of his [Fish's] critique are therefore radical: Nothing, so to speak, can be ruled out – not religious orthodoxy or even theocracy' (Owen, 1999, p. 913). Such sentences count as a CPL; there are others:

> Contemporary political theorists have debated at great length the consequences of the demise of liberal rationalism for politics, but a crucial aspect has been neglected. (Owen, 1999, p. 912)

> Little has been written directly on the significance of the demise of liberal rationalism for the liberal doctrines on religion ... (Owen, 1999, p. 912)

> Following antifoundationalism all the way, Fish argues, means giving up on all such projects of overarching and neutral inclusion. What does this mean for religious freedom and the separation of church and state? (Owen, 1999, p. 912)

Sentences like the above provide a contrast to summaries proffered in the preceding paragraphs. As shown in earlier chapters, CPLs follow SPLs, for before an idea, a body of results or a school of thought can be critiqued, the content of the things that are being critiqued have to be made available, for logical reasons. Again, before something can be critiqued, that something has to be introduced. That is the function of a SPL. But if existing literature was sufficient, then there would be no need to rehash what is already known. New articles and new books are written precisely because another author believes that he or she can reframe the debate, challenge obsolete findings, and provide a new way of thinking about a problem. And that is what

CPLs do: they highlight limitations and deficiencies in previous works in some systematic and cogent way, which leads to a GAP. The excerpts above illustrate the CPLs/GAPs shown in earlier chapters that function as a way of providing a rationale for the current paper without being as explicit as social science journal articles. How will Owen remedy the GAP that follows from the CPLs?

> I offer a limited defense of liberalism against Fish's critique. I will begin by showing how Fish reaches his radical conclusions. I will then argue that, despite his shockingly antiliberal conclusions, Fish remains entangled within the liberal worldview he is so intent on criticizing ... I conclude that Fish has underestimated the conceptual and moral power of liberalism. This underestimation is largely the result of mistakenly identifying neutrality as the essence of liberalism ... (Owen, 1999, p. 913)

In the excerpt above, Owen provides readers with an itinerary of what he will do in the paper; therefore, that paragraph would count as a WTD, similar to the ones we have examined thus far in social science journal articles. The paragraph above captures the main (research) question that the author is posing in the text. In social science journal articles, those questions are resolved by collecting and analyzing data, then presenting the results. However, in certain review articles, theoretical articles, and philosophy articles, there are no palpable data that are analyzed. Instead, the new claims and results occur as a result of argumentation. Owen spends pages challenging Fish's presuppositions about liberalism, his conclusions, and the logical consequents of his claim if assumed to be true. In other words, Owen uses Professor Fish's writings as data and attempts to use them as POC, as a way of setting up his own argument to emerge. Owen's new 'findings' will be comparable to the ROFs we have seen in earlier chapters, except that the claims emerge from the critiques of previous arguments rather than some 'empirical' data. An argument is 'any group of propositions of which one is claimed to follow from the others, which are regarded as providing support or grounds for the truth of that one' (Copi & Cohen, 1990, p. 6). What might those 'results' look like? Consider the following sentences:

> We may say, then, that Fish's antiliberalism is just as tolerant, after a fashion, as liberalism. (Owen, 1999, p. 920)

> Liberalism may have a greater hold on Fish than he recognizes. (Owen, 1999, p. 921)

> Fish does not adequately recognize that his antifoundationalism rests entirely on liberal presuppositions. Thus, however antiliberal his aims may be, he remains in the grip of liberalism in subtle yet powerful ways. (Owen, 1999, p. 923)

> Fish thus significantly mistakes the degree or manner of liberalism's opposition to religion. (Owen, 1999, p. 923)

> It is partly for the benefits of such protection [that religion provides to liberalism] of the private sphere that liberalism is worth defending. (Owen, 1999, p. 923)

> Thanks to liberalism, 'culture war' has replaced civil war. For this we must be grateful. (Owen, 1999, p. 923)

> Even one who recognizes the radical limitations of liberalism with a view to the ultimate truth remains morally obligated to uphold liberalism in the absence of a better practicable alternative. (Owen, 1999, p. 923)

Sentences like the ones above do not make a critique of prior works, nor do they point out a gap or a rationale of sorts. They all declare something. We might even call such statements claims and/or conclusions, for such propositions are 'affirmed on the basis of the other propositions of the argument' (Copi & Cohen, 1990, p. 6). That something is the product of the criticisms he has pointed out in previous writings on the topic. Grammatically, the arrival of conclusions is signaled by conclusion markers such as 'therefore,' 'hence,' 'thus,' 'as a result,' 'for such reasons,' etc. The claims Owen makes are new – claims that emerge and grow out of the previous claims made by Fish, whose own claims emerge out of those who asserted prior claims. This type of process – claim→critique of claim→new claim – is what the business of academia and scholarship is all about, for disagreements about and challenges to a claim spur on others to modify and remedy the initial claim (Fish, 1980). This constantly evolving cycle of claims-making is aptly described as a dialectical process, for ideas emerge out of other ideas. *Ex nihilo nihil fit.* This logic is applicable to all social science texts – from a PhD dissertation to a research paper in the fourth year of an undergraduate education. The difference between the two preceding examples lies in the scale and sophistication of the projects, not in their underlying form or logic.

Seven paragraphs constitute the introduction in Wyller's (2005) article entitled 'The place of pain in life,' published in *Philosophy*. Before we examine the introduction, one of the notable points about this article is the absence of an abstract. There is no 100–150-word synopsis of what the article is about, a pattern that appears to be rather common in philosophy journals. Readers have no way of perusing the article to discern if indeed it is pertinent to a topic that a student might have chosen to write about. A reader has to wade through the introduction to find out if the article should be included in her literature review.

The second notable observation about articles in philosophy journals, again, is the absence of data and methods, results, and discussion sections.

That absence might be explained by the fact that political theory, literary criticism, and philosophy are disciplines that generally do not collect and analyze data in a social scientific sense. If 'data' are analyzed, they are likely to be texts. Thus, literary critics tend to use the actual writings of novelists, philosophers, and other authors as a corpus of data to be analyzed. And because no 'data' exist in the sense that social scientists are accustomed to, the character of the 'results' that are produced is likely to be different. The 'results' found (what I have termed ROF in social science articles) are more likely to be arguments that an author makes to challenge the arguments made by a previous scholar, thus building on previous knowledge and providing a new claim. This pattern was evident in the previous article we examined. Rather than Result of Findings (ROF), we could anticipate that philosophy's equivalent of an ROF might be Result of Argumentation (ROA). But aside from the absence of an abstract, data and methods, results, and discussion sections, are there other similarities and differences between articles in philosophy journals and articles in social science journals?

To illustrate how articles in philosophy journals are organized, I have chosen to work backwards this time, much like the way a homicide detective works backward to reconstruct a crime scene and discern a victim's last-seen-alive location. Like a particularly difficult logic problem or a murder investigation, sometimes, we have to assume the conclusion to be false and then proceed to attempt to prove it as a way of finding the truth.

So what does Wyller (2005) want to claim as the 'news' in 'The place of pain in life'? – the new claim that he is making in his paper in a way that is sufficiently different from those of previous scholars who have written on the topic of pain? The answer emerges in the very end. Wyller begins the last paragraph by returning to the principal author he is pushing against (much like the way Owen pushes against Fish) and critiquing in his paper – John Hyman – and uses the idioms Hyman used as a backdrop for his claims: '(1) I have an itch in my toe; (2) I have a headache; (3) my leg is hurting.' Wyller then goes on to write: 'I accept the structural equivalence ... but I do not agree that (3) is more transparent than (1) and (2).'

There are two points that need to be elaborated. First, that the concept 'transparency' will be meaningful in how the second claim (Wyller) differs from the first (Hyman) one. We might anticipate that the ROA will revolve around the issue of transparency. Second, the two phrases, 'I accept' and 'I agree,' although characteristically different from the language of social science journal articles, perform a similar kind of function noted in previous chapters. 'I accept' is another way of saying that the results (of findings, of argumentation) are consistent with previous findings. Thus, some of the ROAs that Wyller proffers are consistent with the claims previous scholars (e.g., John Hyman) have made. Again, although no 'results' in the social scientific sense are presented, there is conceptual equivalence if we substitute 'findings' with 'argumentation.'

Philosophers do not generally collect data like social scientists do; instead, the data are the texts and arguments that previous scholars have made. Therefore, the phrase 'I do not agree' should be seen for its fraternal resemblance to Results to the Contrary (RTC). If we substitute 'argumentation' for 'results,' then we can see that Wyller is presenting an argument that contradicts and is inconsistent with previous findings. So what is Wyller's new claim? He writes, 'If I had to choose, I would say (1) and (2) are more transparent; making explicit what is implied by (3) as well: a feeling person.' Then in the last sentence, readers are finally treated to a new claim, an ROA of sorts: 'Thus whereas Hyman takes pains to be modes of person's limbs, I propose we understand them as modes of persons located in their limbs.'

As one might suspect, the difference between the two assertions appears to be minute; but then again, I am not in a position to assess the merits and significance of such assertions, for I am insufficiently trained in that discipline to be able to even appreciate the magnitude of the difference. But, if we presuppose that 'modes of person's limbs' and 'modes of persons located in their limbs' are not that radically different, then Wyller has done what social scientists also do in their journal articles: present a claim that is sufficiently new – not a paradigm-shifting one – to warrant peer reviewers to accept its contribution to the literature by voting to publish the paper. One might say that Wyller simply made a quarter turn.

We began by working backwards. We already know Wyller's conclusion, his new claim, but what question did he ask in order to arrive at his conclusion? Wyller (2005, p. 385) begins the article in the following way: 'I take a hammer, drive a nail into the wall and suddenly hit my left thumb. I spontaneously withdraw my hand, screaming. Where is the pain located?' Wyller contextualizes that primary question in the work of John Hyman's article entitled 'Pains and places,' and it is against that previous work and theorist that Wyller is pushing. He also critiques Hyman's work as a way of justifying the necessity of his own paper: 'However, I believe he overstates his point to the effect of excluding some natural allies. Hyman is right that the pain of my thumb is in my thumb. But Wittgensteinian expressivists are also right that it is where I, the whole person, am.'

Wyller's contention with previous work is that it insufficiently locates the experience of pain (CPL); he wants expanded coverage of where pain is located and experienced. And by turning 'our attention to the fact of embodied consciousness,' Wyller will propose in his current paper to remedy the limitations that exist in the philosophy of pain literature. This notion is the rationale (RAT) of his paper, but notice that such justifications and itineraries are not stated explicitly; the reader, again, must do the work of inferring one or two steps in the reading process, work that does not have to be performed in social science journals. Without a sufficient background understanding of the pain literature, or a sound understanding of the extra work that readers have to perform, an undergraduate student reading this type of an article is apt to get lost in the inference that has to be made during reading.

The term 'embodied consciousness' not only provides an implicit rationale of his work but also hints at the literature to be reviewed as a way of setting up his argument. As a way of summarizing previous literature (SPL), and true to the identity of the discipline, the author begins his setting up of connecting parts to the whole by introducing the work of Aristotle; he then connects the concept of autopoiesis to Aristotle before presenting the material basis of consciousness. The author then brings in Kant and Wittgenstein as a way of prepping the reader to his line of argumentation: 'I thus suggest we take the autopoietic whole/part relation as the key to understanding phantom pains' (p. 393). Consider why phantoms would be problematic, and the most difficult test for the question he has asked. Explaining pain in one's thumb as a result of an accidental hammer blow can be accounted for, whether the pain is located in the thumb, the mind, or the nervous system. The pain is 'real.' It really hurts. Phantom pains that occur from missing limbs, however, are a bit problematic to explain. He has to show that answer through argumentation rather than data collection:

> Within today's natural sciences one encounters definitions of 'life' in terms of physiology, thermodynamics, information theory, biochemistry and genetics. No unified conception is to be found. However, this also makes it a legitimate task for anyone to reflect upon which one among the vast definitions best captures the distinction we naturally draw between living and non-living things. (p. 387)

That is why Wyller has to incorporate all of the preceding hard sciences in order to answer his question. Trying to account for pains in missing limbs is much more difficult to do than trying to explain the pain in an attached thumb. To provide sufficient background knowledge (SPL), the author has to go outside of the discipline and draw on the work done in natural sciences to buttress his claims. Whether one goes outside of a discipline or stays inside, synthesis of the literature prior to a critique of it entails a tremendous amount of reduction and condensation. Writers have to find a way to boil down numerous themes that a topic has been grouped into and repeat that process for their own work. Synthesis in philosophy also occurs along a parallel line. One must consult and review canonic authors, and apply their obscure ideas to suit one's aims in a paper. This practice of finding new concepts and then explaining and justifying their relevance for the proposed work is one way in which theoretical papers differ from research papers. In such papers, existing ideas are redefined, reframed, and commandeered to produce a new idea, much like the way Wyller uses biological concepts to define the concept of life, and then apply it for his purposes in his paper on pain. In research papers, the 'new angle' is the empirical data that are analyzed, not novel ideas.

There is also one final noteworthy difference between social science articles and philosophical articles. In the former, authors begin the process of future scholarship in the present by proffering the limitations of their own studies and works. Such self-critique paves the way for future research that can be carried out by others. As we have seen, Recommendations for Future Works (RFWs) also perform a similar task of suggesting a path of improvement for future scholars and research; in the philosophy articles we examined, we have seen that the reader must come up with a POC and RPP without much help from the author. There are no benign recommendations that are made to future authors in the philosophical works we have seen thus far. Scholars have to read between the lines to find the GAPs and CPLs, and come up with an implicit RAT. This difficulty is compounded by the lack of repetition of essential components. In other words, this lack of repetition leads to readers being left on their own during the reading process. For an undergraduate or a beginning graduate student trying to read between the lines for the first time, that is a tall order.

So far, I have argued that there are parallels between social science texts and philosophy texts for the simple reason that scholarship tends to be dialectical in character. We have seen throughout this book that social scientists, political theorists, and philosophers begin their works by introducing a body of previous thoughts (SPL) which is then critiqued (CPL) as a way of highlighting some missing dimension in the literature (GAP). This absence, explicitly and implicitly, provides a paper's necessary existential justification (RAT). In this section, I want to apply the reading codes to one of the books that shaped my undergraduate education. Will the reading codes be applicable to one of the most influential philosophical works in the past 100 years, thereby buttressing the claims I have made in this book, or will the RCOS fall flat on its face and show it to be nothing more than feces smeared on the walls of the academy?

Rawls (1971, pp. vii–viii) begins the preface to his book *A Theory of Justice* in the following way in the second paragraph:

(1) Perhaps I can best explain my aim in this book as follows. (2) During much of modern moral philosophy the predominant systematic theory has been some form of utilitarianism. (3) One reason for this is that it has been espoused by a long line of brilliant writers who have built up a body of

thought truly impressive in its scope and refinement. (4) We sometimes forget that the great utilitarians, Hume and Adam Smith, Bentham and Mill, were social theorists and economists of the first rank; (5) and the moral doctrine they worked out was framed to meet the needs of their wider interests and to fit into a comprehensive scheme. (6) Those who criticized them often did so on a much narrower front. (7) They pointed out the obscurities of the principle of utility and noted the apparent incongruities between many of its implications and our moral sentiments. (8) But they failed, I believe, to construct a workable and systematic moral conception to oppose it. (9) The outcome is that we often seem forced to choose between utilitarianism and intuitionism. (10) Most likely we finally settle upon a variant of the utility principle circumscribed and restricted in certain ad hoc ways by intuitionistic constraints. (11) Such a view is not irrational; (12) and there is no assurance that we can do better. (13) But this is no reason not to try.

How do we make sense of a block of text like this? What is the author trying to do in this paragraph? Sentence #1 appears to do the work of a WTD, but we are not sure exactly what Rawls will do in his book. So what is he trying to do? Sentence #2 introduces what the paragraph will be about. Moreover, Rawls tells readers that one particular form of philosophy has been the 'predominant' one. Sentences #2–5 provide what is aptly termed an SPL, for Rawls is summarizing previous works; sentences #3–5 elaborate on the prior scholars who have written on the topic (Hume, Smith, Bentham, Mill), their influence, and prior attempts at constructing a 'comprehensive' scheme of sorts. Sentences #6–7 provide an SPL of the CPL that has been made in previous works as well; that is, Rawls provides readers with a thematically organized classification in SPL form of the CPL. So what is that critique?

Rawls notes that the implications of utilitarian theory are not consistent with a person's own sense of morality. What does this sentence mean? If, for example, we had to kill one innocent person to save the lives of a hundred people, would that decision be morally justifiable? In its most simplistic version of utilitarianism, the guiding principle of the greatest good for the greatest number of people would justify that decision to violate the fundamental rights of one person. In its most obtuse form, that is what utilitarianism and democracy are. And from sentences #1–7 what Rawls has done is provide an SPL and a thematically organized SPL of the CPL – a summary of previous works and critiques.

But beginning sentence #8 with the words 'But they failed' suggests that he will provide a CPL of his own. As we saw in Chapter 4, such disjunction markers portend contrasts to emerge (e.g., 'I like you, but ...'). So what is Rawls's CPL? That there is an absence of a systematic method to oppose the morally unpalatable outcomes illustrated in the hypothetical example. Such an assertion constitutes a GAP. If the dominant form of philosophy has been utilitarianism, and, according to its tenets, distasteful outcomes are justified on practical and democratic grounds, and there is no cogent and systematic moral argument that could be made against such practices, except a nagging sense of intuition that such practices violate some pre-existing sense of morality, and only 'ad hoc' ways of settling such questions exist, then what ought to be done? Can Rawls do any better than intuition-ism and ad hoc ways of countering such outcomes? He says there's no guarantee, that there is 'No assurance that we can do better. But this is no reason not to try.'

The preceding declaration is not a very forcefully argued RAT. Imagine if someone asked Rawls why his *A Theory of Justice* was necessary. He has obviously identified a GAP in the literature, but rather than assuredly pro-nouncing the necessity of his work, he provides the response noted above. Another way of illustrating the rhetorical equivalence of Rawls's answer is to imagine a girl who demands of a teenage boy that he provide her with a good rationale as to why she should go out with him. His answer is the following: 'If you don't want to go out with me, that wouldn't be irrational. There is no assurance that I can do better than your previous boyfriends. But that is no reason not to go out with me.' Such an answer is tentative, weak, and some-thing that only a George McFly or a Leonard Hofstadter would utter. One would be tempted to donate money to such a person so that he can go buy a loaf of self-confidence. Perhaps, Rawls is just being humble. Consider how the next paragraph is organized:

(1) What I have attempted to do is to generalize and carry to a higher order of abstraction the traditional theory of the social contract as represented by Locke, Rousseau, and Kant. (2) In this way I hope that the theory can be developed so that it is no longer open to the more obvious objections often thought fatal to it. (3) Moreover, this theory seems to offer an alterna-tive systematic account of justice that is superior, or so I argue, to the dominant utilitarianism of the tradition. (4) The theory that results is highly Kantian in nature. (5) Indeed, I must disclaim any originality for the views I put forward. (6) The leading ideas are classical and well known. (7) My intention has been to organize them into a general framework by using certain simplifying devices so that their full force can be appreciated. (8) My ambitions for the book will be completely realized if it enables one to see more clearly the chief structural features of the alternative concep-tion of justice that is implicit in the contract tradition and points the way to its further elaboration. (9) Of the traditional views, it is this conception, I believe, which best approximates our considered judgments of justice and constitutes the most appropriate moral basis for a democratic society. (Rawls, 1971, p. viii)

If one uttered the semantic equivalent of a spate of talk like the preceding paragraph on the street, it would, necessarily, have to be followed by an 'Oh Snap!' or 'Three snaps in a circle!' Here's why. If Hume, Bentham, Smith, and Mill count as the previous authors who have championed utilitarian theories of the social contract (SPL), then Locke, Rousseau, and Kant constitute the previous authors who might be classified as influential proponents of a deontological theory of social contract (SPL). Rawls is summarizing and critiquing two of the most influential schools of thought in Western philosophy for the past 500 years. Rather than relying on 'ad hoc' explanations and 'intuitionism,' as others before him have done (CPL), Rawls is proposing that he can come up with a theory of society that is general (as opposed to intuitionistic) and systematic (as opposed to ad hoc) (RAT). He is proclaiming that his theory of society and justice will be 'superior' to those of prevailing utilitarianism and of a 'higher order' than previous theories proffered by theorists such as Locke, Rousseau, and Kant. That is like a rookie boxer telling Mike Tyson, Mohammed Ali, and Joe Frazier that he can box better than them. Either one is crazy to say stuff like that, or Rawls really has an unrivaled left hook.

In sentence #4 when Rawls states that his new theory is 'highly Kantian in nature' and in sentence #6 he claims that 'The leading ideas are classical and well known,' he is introducing the reader to the background literature (SPL), for those three words (leading, classical, well known) mean nearly the same thing. And because Rawls is using ideas that already exist in one form or another, perhaps that is why he humbly disclaims any originality. But notice how the form and movement of Rawls's ideas have been shaped by prior research. Political theorists throughout the centuries have attempted to provide a coherent narrative of how a society secures a unified and stable social order composed of free and equal citizens despite fundamental differences in their moral, philosophical, and religious views. Such a task is easy when a society is composed of angels, for values such as equality, piety, and justice would be abundant, and blindly assuming them as a necessary psychological precondition is not problematic. Governments would require minimal use of coercion. Or, as Durkheim would hypothesize, minor offenses would rise to the level of capital offenses even in a society of angels.

The problem for political theorists has been that such benign assumptions have to be set aside and the empirical realities of a pluralistic world have to be presupposed from the beginning. That is, robbers, thieves, rapists, child molesters, and murderers would also dwell in the midst of angels, and they would have to be included in any theory of the state in order for it to be truly universalizable and logically consistent – *reductio ad absurdum*. Hence, Kant assumed as a premise for his political (and ethical) theory a state that could be constructed through mutual agreement even by a 'nation of devils':

> In order to organize a group of rational beings who together require univer-
> sal laws for their survival, but of whom each separate individual is secretly
> inclined to exempt himself from them, the constitution must be so designed
> that, although the citizens are opposed to one another in their private atti-
> tudes, these opposing views may inhibit one another in such a way that the
> public conduct of the citizens will be the same as if they did not have such
> evil attitudes. (Kant, [1784] 1991, pp. 112–13)

To accommodate the existence of such vagaries of character and disposition
in the self and theoretical framework, political theorists since the time of
Locke, Rousseau, and Kant have pursued a definition of justice that is devoid
of substantive content, toward a purely formal and procedural account (Fish,
1999). When Rawls states that his theory is 'highly Kantian,' he is summarizing, compressing, and reducing Kant's idea of mutual consent as a
legitimating principle, principle of self-interest, and the categorical impera-
tive as necessary preconditions for a theory of a social contract into one
word – 'Kantian.' If readers do not understand the weight of the word 'Kantian'
and its impact, they are likely to miss other connections to previous theorists
in the chapters to come. One word does all that work.

What does Rawls mean when he says 'I have attempted to generalize and
carry to a higher order of abstraction the traditional theory of the social contract?' This tendency toward abstraction and generality is evident in Rawls's
notion of the 'veil of ignorance' within 'the original position.' The original
position is, according to Rawls (1971, p.12), the 'appropriate initial status
quo' and serves as a theoretical underpinning of the two principles of justice
that would be chosen by all rational persons. In this fictitious account, subjects are to devise social and public policy that would be mutually agreed to
by all members of society – including the rapists and child molesters. The aim
is to recreate one of the fundamental moments in the origins of society and
the social contract: to address the problem of difference and self-interest, to
prevent any one subject from choosing policies that show preference for one
group within society, the subjects are hidden behind a veil of ignorance where
any identifying markers such as race, class, and gender, and hence, bias and
preference, would exert little influence on the adoption of public policy. The
'simplifying devices' he refers to in sentence #7 describe conceptual tools he
has modified and developed from previous scholars.

One can see the genealogical and conceptual debt that Rawls owes to previous scholars. In a way, Rawls's work is the culmination, synthesis, and
apogee of Western philosophical thought, for he draws upon Descartes'
([1641] 1951) epistemological certitude as a metaphysical attribute and
mooring for his 'reflective equilibrium'; he relies on Mill's (1997) principle of
utilitarianism as a second principle of justice ('maximum minimum'); he pre-
supposes difference as a potential cause of conflict that ought to be set aside

in public domains *à la* Locke or curtailed through the despotic pronouncements of a bureaucratic Leviathan *à la* Hobbes; he uses logical consistency, universalizability, and mutual consent as necessary criteria for a rule's applicability (Kant [1784], 1991). The word 'sinuous' captures the winding history and summary of political thought quite well. Another word sums up Professor Rawls's *A Theory of Justice*: genius.

If Professor Rawls's final argument is brilliant, the general method of arriving at that destination is less so, for the road that he traveled is a road that all academic writers must traverse. As Professor Rawls admits, he does not have original ideas of his own. That is partially true. He has simply borrowed and modified the previous ideas to make his argument. He wrote the book because he saw that there was a GAP in the existing state of the literature in political philosophy, and he could remedy that GAP. That GAP served as his RAT. But before he could remedy that GAP, hundreds of pages are spent summarizing (SPL) and critiquing (CPL) the previous scholars who have written on the subject. Then the results of his arguments (ROA) are presented. In this sense, the form of the arguments made in humanities and social sciences is not that different. They have an underlying structure and form.

The Form of the Reading Codes

As I have argued in this book, social science journal articles tend to be organized along the structures I have described. Again, before one can write a research paper, an article, or a book, the author must be able to justify why his or her proposed work is warranted. That rationale is shaped by the deficiencies in the current state of the literature. If there are no flaws, deficiencies, or limitations – perfection – in the knowledge base (literature), why would anyone try to improve it? Perfection, by definition, necessitates no change. Academics and scholars do so because they believe that they can improve the state of the knowledge by redefining and reframing the research questions posed in the discipline, or by challenging the methods and procedures that a previous researcher used. At times, the improvement that results is spectacular and paradigm-shifting; the agents of such change become superstars in their disciplines; most of the time, the improvement is minute, but sufficiently innovative to warrant publication. I think I have also shown that that general pattern holds in non-social-sciences as well.

I must admit that trying to use the RCOS on a 500-page text is a formidable task. However, if readers use the highlighter and pen to highlight the important parts of a book, then the task becomes a bit more manageable. I argued that in social science journal articles, the ROF and GAP are two of the most important nuggets of information that ought to be highlighted, for the simple reason that the ROF readily provides an answer to the question, 'What did they find?' and ROFs become SPLs in a future paper. GAP is important for the reason that it answers the 'So what?' question. If an author can't answer this question, then that paper ought not to be attempted, or the author should read more. But I presume that students reading this book, for the most part anyway, will not have to worry about applying the RCOS to a 500-page book. Even I would not assign such an asinine task to my students.

I would, however, assign students to read a 20–30-page journal article and verify their correct application of the reading codes. As I have argued again and again, this project was motivated by the simple fact that I saw recurring errors in students' papers; when I looked back on my career as a student, I noticed that I had made the same errors. I just wanted to find a way to correct them. Although I began with the assumption that writing problems can be remedied by sending students to writing centers, I found this solution to be incorrect. Students' writing problems existed on several levels. Writing problems that were rooted at the conceptual level affected papers on a structural level, which then seeped into mechanical details. Simply fixing sentences and grammar did not work to improve students' writing at all. Rather than examining badly written papers to try to fix them, I changed my assumptions and decided to examine well-written papers to learn how to write them so that I could teach those techniques to students. 'Where would I find well-written papers?', I thought to myself. Then I looked around my office. Duh.

I began to read social science articles and attempted to understand the text at two levels: (1) 'What is the author trying to do in this paragraph, this sentence?' and (2) 'How is this article structurally organized?' Once I started asking those questions, I began to notice a recurring pattern in the way the journal articles were written. Readers will have noticed that the reading codes are represented in a rather odd combination of – sometimes vowel-less – consonant clusters: WTD, ROF, SPL, CPL. Those codes serve as evidence that I had indeed asked the first question as a guiding principle in the current project. I began the reading codes by writing out 'what they do,' 'results of findings,' 'summary of previous literature,' etc. in the margins and found them to be too cumbersome and unwieldy to write each and every time (i.e., the EEECA model and the SQ3R model). So I just started using the acronyms of the functions performed in the text. After about two years of reading, I began to see a pattern in the way the articles are structurally organized. SPLs generally preceded CPLs and GAPs; RTCs and RCLs generally appeared in the back of articles rather than in the front and so on. I also noticed what the authors weren't doing in their papers. For example, some authors I was reading Missed an Obvious Point (MOP) in their discussions;

I noticed the authors claimed something that ought not to have been claimed, and those became Points of Critique (POC) I could use in a future paper. Sometimes, a point that an author missed was a Relevant Point to Pursue (RPP) in a future paper. These became the reading strategy codes.

Once I formulated a preliminary RCOS, I asked several of my colleagues to try it out on a journal article. For about a year, I pleaded, entreated, and begged them to try it on their own readings. After little success, I did what most professors would probably do: I made the undergraduate students try reading with the RCOS. I spent two hours reading one article with the entire class to demonstrate how it worked. I think the codes worked. In the final research papers students submitted, I did not find gross structural problems in their papers. There were other typical errors (e.g., capitalization, fragments, semicolon abuse, etc.) but those were problems that could now be fixed rather easily. Encouraged by the success, I tried it with a graduate class. I met with moderate success. A colleague (Dr Brian Cutler) who was teaching a professional seminar asked me to talk about my ongoing research. I asked if I could share with the students the reading codes. He obliged. Afterwards, he suggested that I write a book. I thought he was joking.

It has been over three years since *How to Read Journal Articles in the Social Sciences* was first published. Each time I have taught a fourth-year capstone course and used the book to introduce the reading codes to students, as a way of reading critically and organizing their notes to be used in the writing process, the students ask a simple question that always takes me by surprise: 'Why didn't we learn this in our first year?' My response is that I do not teach first-year courses. When I asked if this method of reading would have been helpful in their first year in college, they replied that their performance in school would have been different had they learned how to read properly. I tend to be very suspicious of people in general so I have to take such assertions with a grain of salt. However, I have received several random e-mails from students who have used the book, and told me how helpful the reading codes have been in their own work – how confident they felt after reading with the codes. Some students' experiences have not been so positive.

As stated in Chapter 6, there have been students who have struggled with reading journal articles using the reading codes and writing their research papers using the RCOS. There may be several reasons why students do not react favorably to the reading codes and the research papers that are expected of them. First, students may not be used to the sheer volume of reading (a minimum of 30 journal articles) required for their research papers. Second, they may not be used to active and careful reading, having read only the introductions and conclusions of journal articles in previous coursework. (Students related that this strategy was commonly used to obtain quotable material from a journal article.) Third, the expectation of an original claim/finding/argument may be stressful for students who are accustomed to writing papers that only require summarizing the work of others. Fourth, students just hate being in my class; they have tried to get out but are stuck because all other sections are closed. Consequently, they just tune out. Fifth, some students do not adjust well to change.

As Alfred Adler (1917) noted, new situations reveal a person's true personality, and lead to neurotic failures if the new situation is traumatic enough and wounds one's pride sufficiently. The enormity of the readings, the repetitiveness of the RCOS, the mechanics of writing, the expectation of a new claim – new situations – have led to stress, anxiety, failures, and sometimes, breakdowns. In those moments, I can only sympathize with what the students are going through. I have been there myself. However, the deadline for, and the expectation of, a competently executed paper does not go away. That expectation is relentlessly brutal and persistent – just like a landlord's expectation of monthly rent, a tax bill from the Internal Revenue Service/Canada Revenue Agency, and a stomach's wont to be satiated daily. Just as importantly, successes do not define one's mettle as a scholar. It is how we react to failures that defines our scholarly character. That same lesson applies to students who have failed a course for the first time; a junior faculty member whose paper has been rejected by a journal for the umpteenth time; or a senior professor whose book has been ripped to pieces by reviewers.

8

Concluding Remarks

Although I have heard the phrase 'television makes you stupid' countless times, I have never heard the phrase 'reading makes you stupid.' In the latter, reading makes you stupid only if you read stupid stuff, but, even in this view, the act of reading is not dismissed as a worthless activity. The two phrases, however, serve as a good contrast between the two mediums through which people know. One is word-based and the other is purportedly picture-based. One requires audiences to process and digest syntactically complex sentences, and follow a linear and carefully crafted sequential flow of ideas, propositions, and arguments, the other requires a couch.

The two types of medium – television and book – are what Postman (1985) refers to as *telegraphic* and *typographic* forms of epistemology. The telegraphic mind requires plain language to understand and enjoy television, language that is syntactically simple, with minimal logical propositions, assertions, and arguments. Such discourse is illogical, emotional, and expressive; it is banal in every sense of the word, and pollutes public communication. The typographic mind, on the other hand, requires language that is logical, sequential, linear, and orderly. Such language is the language of Shakespeare, Aristotle, Plato, and the rest of the great Western Classics authors. Consequently, literary language is aesthetic, a pleasure to read, and fertilizing, but, more importantly, it produces virtuous traits in the reader.

Postman values the typographic mind over the telegraphic one because of the type of minds that reading literary words produces. Reading requires that readers follow a linear and carefully crafted sequential flow of ideas and arguments and, for Postman (1985, p. 51), that is what reading does: 'uncover lies, confusions and overgeneralizations, to detect abuses of logic and commonsense.' For Postman a culture that is 'dominated by print' is predisposed to a mind-set characterized by a 'coherent, orderly arrangement of facts and ideas' in its public discourse (p. 51). Pictures, images, and plain language needed to understand television, on the other hand, do not require complex sentences and logical argumentation for 'discourse is conducted largely through visual imagery, which is to say that television gives us conversation in images, not words' (p. 7).

Postman's charge is that television makes too much information available and, hence, renders it useless. Postman argues that superfluous information is useless because newly received information has no relevance to the audience's immediate life: information becomes context free, not bound to anyone's particular history, setting, and time, but free-floating, with no clear mooring, captured in catchy phrases and bites. According to Postman, television is primarily for entertainment; it has nothing to teach us, in form or content; moreover, it does so in a plain and vulgar way: 'what we watch is a medium [television] which presents information in a form that renders it simplistic, non-substantive, non-historical and non-contextual; that is to say, information packaged as entertainment' (p. 141).

Postman argues for television's evilness because of the type of minds it creates; people who watch television want constant amusement, and that desire for a never-ending good time is likely to lead to 'death.' The death is probably not literal, but it is accurate in another sense. Those who watch excessive amounts of television, Postman would say, do not read; moreover, they rarely do anything else, such as play sports, go out for walks, or do chores around the house. The word reserved in our culture for such persons is 'couch potato.' And if Postman's characterization of television is right, then in the long run, this culture would breed nothing but couch potatoes; but more significantly, people would turn into mental couch potatoes as well because not only would they lack the physical capabilities to exercise their bodies but also muscles that work the mind would have atrophied due to inactivity. The death in Postman's work is mental and intellectual – in the mind – but it is every bit as scary as physical death.

Postman is interested in the effects of language. The effects he wants are virtuous ones, and in reading literary 'printed words,' the effects are twofold: one benefits from the activity of reading itself since it teaches the reader to 'uncover lies, confusions, overgeneralizations, to detect abuses of logic and common sense'; the other benefit is that readers undergo a profound aesthetic experience. According to Postman, reading literary works leads to critical thinking and aesthetic appreciation. Postman is correct to point out that reading produces a certain type of mind; however, the texts that are read as a way of cultivating one's mind or for enjoyment do not give birth to themselves. The authors of those texts, wittingly and carefully, craft a linear and sequential flow of ideas and arguments, or unwittingly scatter their texts with lies, confusion, abuses of logic and common sense.

Put another way, although the reader and the writer may be separated by time and distance, they stand face to face in intimate ways. They are bound to one another because writers are engaged with their readers the moment they think about a potential writing project to the time they compose it and complete it. Linear and logical arguments do not emerge on their own; they are created by writers who assume the role of readers, who, although invisible and absent, exert exponential force in the shape of an author's argument (Eco, 1979). Good writers anticipate readers' reactions and rebuttals even before they emerge, and craft their ideas with such responses in mind. That type of sensitivity and care can be seen in the way paragraphs are organized, for responsible authors lead their readers to 'see' their train of thought and the logic that got them there; those types of paragraphs flow 'tightly' and can't be undone by simply moving one paragraph to another location. If one of those paragraphs is moved, then the entire argument would collapse under its own weight. Irresponsible writers, on the other hand, are similar to bad lovers, for they are inconsiderate of their partners during their intimate acts. Both do as they please without an iota of thought for their bored partners.

As I have shown in this book, some authors prepare their readers much better than others – by logically and sensitively guiding them through abstract points and tricky curves. For such reasons, reading and writing are intersubjective acts, for readers and writers enter into a mutually pleasurable yet arduous task of creating and reading texts together. Writers have readers in mind when crafting their ideas and structure of arguments; readers have the authors in mind as they attempt to understand the intent, purpose, and aim of a particular block of text. That is what makes reading and writing dialogic and intersubjective acts, for authors are trying to persuade their readers to see their point; similarly, readers are trying to discern an author's argument and logic as to why he or she organized the text in a particular way or chose a certain word to describe something when another would have sufficed. Texts that are constructed and interpreted in a particular way are not random outcomes. They are collaboratively and reflexively produced by the reader and writer alike – across time, history, and geography – even if they meet for the first time in 500 years. Television requires no such dialogical imagination.

Hence, I have argued that reading and writing, although usually done solitarily, are intersubjective acts. When scholars read the work of a previous scholar, the reader is, in essence, engaged in a silent dialogue with the writer; conversely, the author is engaged in an invisible dialogue with the reader, trying to figure out how best to persuade him to her point of view and accept the validity of her argument. That is what authors are thinking when they are writing. Such a process is aptly termed dialogical. Those types of internal debates that occur between readers and writers are rarely boring and never lonely. I have heard some students and academics complain that scholarly work is lonely, but such a conclusion is drawn because they have conflated solitariness with loneliness. They are not the same things.

Reading for pleasure is done solitarily, primarily for intensely selfish and philosophical ends. The literary critic Harold Bloom (2000, p. 24) advises that before readers engage in activism of any kind – the 10,000 -isms that populate university campuses catering to the just-awakened moral palates of college students – as a result of reading a particular text, they ought to set aside such defiant notions until the author is first 'discovered': 'Do not attempt to improve your neighbor or your neighborhood by what or how you read.' That is Bloom's second principle of reading. And for Bloom, and other literary critics of his variety, we ought to read in 'quest of a mind more original than our own' (p. 25), to strengthen ourselves. Pleasure reading in such a view is not social. One might even call such an act the epitome of antisociality.

In the context of social science reading and writing, however, I have argued for their intersubjectivity purely on formal grounds. Throughout this book I have also argued for the intersubjective character of social science writing by demonstrating how the very content of social science articles exemplify and reify that sociality. We saw this tendency in the front and rear of journal articles. Authors entered the scholarly community by introducing and discussing the work of previous researchers in abstracts, introductions, and literature reviews. The very research questions asked are shaped by the history of a discipline. This practice, in and of itself, attests to the heavy intellectual down-payments scholars have to make in order to establish residency in a community of scholars. Again, even before scholars can present their own findings, even before they can justify why their proposed works are necessary, the work that preceded theirs must be acknowledged and critiqued before a deficiency in the current state of the literature is remedied. By recognizing, including, discussing, and critiquing previous works, we enter into the socio-moral order of scholarship, for we acknowledge our conceptual debt to those who preceded us in the form of paragraphs and citations.

Discussions and conclusions also illustrated that order and dialogical character of academic work, for results of findings were rarely interpreted and discussed in absolute terms, but always relative to the past findings of previous scholars. Moreover, our contribution is shaped by previous scholars in the discipline who have asked similar questions, used similar methods to answer those questions, and interpreted those results in accordance with a canonic school of thought. That is why knowledge claims grow out of the claims of others: they are conceptually, methodologically, analytically, and temporally bound to the dialectical character of academic scholarship. Knowledge claims do not – cannot – emerge from nothingness. Such debt is paid in the form of citations.

Finally, social science writing embodies and cultivates a selfless moral virtue. That value is manifest in the outward critique in the front of journal articles and an inward one near the end. As we have seen, most, if not all, authors of social science journal articles discuss the limitations of their own work, as well as make recommendations for future works. As I argued in this book, those types of assertions dramatize the gaps in current knowledge. Such self-critiques also illustrate the tenuous and indeterminate character of knowledge claims and knowledge in general in the social sciences. That is to say, there is always room for improvement. Such a humble and skeptical outlook is desirable, for it reifies and parallels professed values in science (not literature), and stylistically prevents an accidental death that hubris might cause (e.g., Icarus). That such a noble moral value is encoded in the structural organization of social science texts sets it apart from other genres (e.g., romance novels, poetry). The moral trajectory of scholarship in the social sciences bends toward humility, and the structure of social science journal articles provides that constraint. That's not a bad thing.

The typographic mind may be desirable to achieve, and colleges and universities are mandated to do it, but there may be less frustrating ways to reach that desirable end, especially in the social sciences. Rather than expecting a desirable trait as an incidental byproduct of the reading process, as Postman does, critical reading ought to be taught to students; they ought to be given tools to spot 'a linear and carefully crafted sequential flow of ideas.' Using social science journal articles and a limited number of non-social science texts, I have shown that academic writing is organized in a very particular way, in a way that is expectable and anticipatable. The sequential, linear, and orderly organization of ideas in social science writing – and non-social science texts – can be canonically formulated as SPL→CPL→GAP→RAT, for that process embodies the structural flow of ideas in social science texts. And rather than simply telling students that there is a pattern in the texts, I have advocated revealing the structure of that pattern in texts so that students can see it, understand it, and – with cautious hope – emulate that pattern in their own writing – before they can be confident enough to overcome their diffidence, and pronounce their own scholarly voice.

As I have argued in this book, reading is not secondary to writing in the social sciences. Reading is half – if not more – of the writing process. The other half entails creative and moral work on the part of students, for they have to find ways of collating, classifying, and organizing previous ideas into highly compressed, yet cogent, thematic categories before they can critique and provide a rationale for their own work. Only then, after the task of organizing and connecting previous ideas is completed, can students compose unique – but limitless – ways of translating those themes into sentences. That task is not easy if the student is honest or obsessively compulsive, and remarkably easy if the student is guileful. As one can see, scholarly writing is a creative and a moral act, but, then again, such exercises of the mind are what a university is principally for – in addition to the cool parties, sports, and, uh, other things best left unsaid – like ice-cold beer.

I began this book with the assumption that writing problems are related to poor reading skills and information management. After ten years of trying to figure out why students were making the types of errors they were making in their papers (e.g., literature reviews, drafts of theses, etc.), I came to the conclusion that students did not have an adequate understanding of the idea of *criticism*. Simply asserting whether one likes the assigned reading or not, or finds it boring, is not a critique. Those are opinions and it is impossible to critique an opinion. Criticisms, on the other hand, are not opinions; they are assessments of a work – whether the work is a painting, film, novel, philosophy book, or a social science article – that are grounded in the normative standards of judgment, which are internal to that discipline. Thus, a test of logical consistency would not – I presume – be particularly relevant for assessing the merits of an oil painting or urban photography; however, for a book on philosophy, it would be a relevant criterion. Similarly, methodological rigor (e.g., random sample selection) would be a poor criterion to use to evaluate the literary merits of a historical novel, but absolutely appropriate for a social science journal article.

That was the problem I noticed again and again in my students' work. They had trouble critiquing the work of the authors they were reading. They were able to summarize, but the idea of critique was not adequately developed. Again, trying to teach critical reading to students who do not know how to do it by telling them to 'read critically' is like trying to instruct aspiring bodybuilders on bodybuilding by telling them to 'go build bodies.' The advice is ridiculously absurd. One would have to tell someone who wants to be a bodybuilder to perform compound movements – exercises that require multiple joints – to develop a solid foundation for the first year or so; then begin to specialize body parts by rotating and cycling training schedules so that each muscle group is targeted a minimum number of times per week. The novice would be instructed to consume one gram of protein or more per pound of body weight, followed by adequate sleep and water intake. Oh, and, uh, avoid beer.

Notice the difference in the quality of instruction that exists between 'go build bodies' and 'perform compound movements, specialize, rotate and cycle, eat proteins, and rest.' The former is completely useless unless one already knows what the directive entails and knows how to do it. When I consulted how-to books to improve writing (literature review), I noticed the general advice that was proffered resembled directives such as 'go build bodies' (SPL). If there were other specific directives that were offered, they were unwieldy and difficult to implement (CPL). I saw that a better way to teach students could be devised (GAP). Consequently, I developed the reading codes as a way of introducing a structure and pattern to the texts students were reading as a way of getting them to engage with them critically (RAT #1). Rather than simply telling students to be 'critical,' this book has provided a way of reading and coding that constitutes the very performance of 'critical reading' others have presupposed (WTDD). I also wanted to find a way for students to organize the information they gathered from the reading codes in some principled and methodical way as a way of getting them to think about the writing process during the act of reading and prewriting, not after (RAT #2). This book has been an attempt to demonstrate to and persuade readers that the reading codes are a relevant and useful heuristic device for critical reading and management of information (WTDD).

I have argued in this book that words, sentences, and paragraphs in social science journal articles perform a particular rhetorical function (ROF), in a way that is expectable and anticipatable according to the structure and logic that is inherent in social science journal writing (ROF). Once readers see this pattern, I argued, they would be able to read in a way that the contents of what they have read can be organized and classified in easily identifiable and retrievable ways. That pattern was introduced as a way of providing textual, cognitive, and conceptual boundaries so that readers did not engage in mindless and meandering reading filled with 'cant' (Bloom, 2000). By identifying the function of texts and marking codes in the margins, I wanted readers to do three things: (1) slow down the act of reading; (2) organize the contents of the reading into recurring themes (e.g., SPL, CPL, GAP, ROF) that can be easily retrieved for writing purposes; and (3) identify potential GAPs so that the reader could anticipate the RAT from the given CPL and GAP for use in their own papers. The advice provided above, I argued, is the reading equivalent of 'perform compound movements, specialize, rotate, cycle, consume protein, and rest.'

The recommendations made in this book are neither radical nor new. I have simply fleshed out what previous writers (e.g., Cone & Foster, 2006; Glatthorn & Joyner, 2005; Rudestam & Newton, 2001; Vipond, 1996) were already doing and have presupposed in their practice (RCL). I have simply reduced their practice and advice into operational and deployable reading codes. This extension is hardly an innovation. In fact, some professors will claim that they already do something like what I have described in their classes. I wouldn't be surprised. That is what my teachers did as well, although they did not call it SPL, CPL, RAT, RCL. Again, that is why I can't take credit for any of the ideas stated here.

Rhetoricians and literary critics – if they read the book at all – will most likely clutch their bellies with near-fatal laughter at the obtusely simplistic analysis of text that I have done here, but, then again, I am not a literary critic trying to break new ground. I may also have forgotten to cite and discuss some of the relevant previous scholars in this area as well. That omission is not attributable to arrogance as much as it is a function of my own pathological ineptitude. And that I have not been able to provide self-critiques and recommendations for future works should not mean that they do not exist. It's just that I am not smart enough to be that critical or reflective. If I were that smart, I'd be a marine biologist or an architect with Vandelay & Associates, but I'm only a teacher.

As a teacher, I have simply attempted to teach students how to read social science journal articles as a way of improving their writing. Also, because I am a teacher, I have a professional obligation to my students, to my institution (employer), and to the discipline to do what is best for my students, irrespective of my personal desire, preference, and inclination to do otherwise. I simply do not matter. That's what being a professional means. For this project, students are and have been the only invisible audience I have had in mind. I hope they will find the reading codes useful, and not hate me when completing the RCOS.

References

Adler, A. (1917). *The Neurotic Constitution: Outlines of a Comparative Individualistic Psychology and Psychotherapy*. (B. Glueck and J. Lind, Trans.) New York: Moffat, Yard, and Company.

Bingenheimer, J., Brennan, R., & Earls, F. (2005). Firearm violence exposure and serious violent behavior. *Science* 308, 1323–6.

Bloom, H. (2000). *How to Read and Why*. New York: Touchstone.

Bui, Y. (2009). *How to Write a Master's Thesis*. Thousand Oaks, CA: Sage.

Cao, L., Adams, A., & Jensen, V. (1997). A test of the black subculture of violence thesis: A research note. *Criminology* 35(2), 367–79.

Canter, D. & Wentink, N. (2004). An empirical test of Holmes and Holmes's serial murder typology. *Criminal Justice and Behavior* 31(4), 489–515.

Canter, D., Alison, L.J., Alison, E. & Wentink, N. (2004). The organized/disorganized typology of serial murder: Myth or model? *Psychology, Public Policy, and Law* 10(3), 293–320.

Cone, J.D. & Foster, S.L. (2006). *Dissertations and Theses: From Start to Finish*. Washington, DC: APA.

Copi, I. & Cohen, C. (1990). *Introduction to Logic*. New York: Macmillan.

Cottrell, S. (2011). *Critical Thinking Skills: Developing Effective Analysis and Argument*. New York: Palgrave Macmillan.

Craswell, G. & Poore, M. (2012). *Writing for Academic Success* (2nd ed.). London: Sage.

Descartes, R. ([1641] 1951). *Meditations on First Philosophy*. New York: Macmillan.

DiCataldo, F. & Everett, M. (2008). Distinguishing juvenile homicide from violent juvenile offending. *International Journal of Offender Therapy and Comparative Criminology* 52(2), 158–74.

Dixon, T.L. & Linz, D. (2000). Race and the misrepresentation of victimization on local television news. *Communication Research* 27(5), 547–73.

Dolan, M. & Smith, C. (2001). Juvenile homicide offenders: 10 years' experience of an adolescent forensic psychiatry service. *The Journal of Forensic Psychiatry* 12(2), 313–29.

Eco, U. (1979). *The Role of the Reader: Explorations in the Semiotics of Texts*. Bloomington, IN: Indiana University Press.

Entman, R. (1990). Modern racism and the images of blacks in local television news. *Critical Studies in Mass Communication* 7, 332–45.

Fink, A. (2010). *Conducting Research Literature Reviews: From the Internet to Paper* (3rd ed.). Thousand Oaks, CA: Sage.

Fish, S. (1980). *Is There a Text in This Class? The Authority of Interpretive Communities*. Cambridge, MA: Harvard University Press.

Fish, S. (1994). *There's No Such Thing as Free Speech … And It's a Good Thing*. Oxford: Oxford University Press.

Fish, S. (1999). *The Trouble with Principle*. Cambridge, MA: Harvard University Press.

Gershenfeld, S. (2014). A review of undergraduate mentoring programs. *Review of Educational Research* 84(3), 365–91.

Glatthorn, A.A. & Joyner, R.L. (2005). *Writing the Winning Thesis or Dissertation: A Step-by-step Guide*. Thousand Oaks, CA: Corwin Press.

Gruenewald, J., Pizarro, J., & Chermak, S. (2009). Race, gender, and the newsworthiness of homicide incidents. *Journal of Criminal Justice* 37, 262–72.

Harris, S.C. (2014). *How to Critique Journal Articles in the Social Sciences*. Thousand Oaks, CA: Sage.

Hattie, J. & Timperley, H. (2007). The power of feedback. *Review of Educational Research* 77(1), 81–112.

Holmes, R.M. & Holmes, S.T. (1994). *Murder in America*. Thousand Oaks, CA: Sage.

Horney, K. (1950). *Neurosis and Human Growth: The Struggle Toward Self-realization*. New York: W.W. Norton.

Hu, S. & Ma, Y. (2010). Mentoring and student persistence in college: A study of the Washington State Achievers Program. *Innovative Higher Education* 35, 329–41.

Jesson, J., Matheson, L., & Lacey, F.M. (2011). *Doing Your Literature Review: Traditional and Systematic Techniques*. London: Sage.

Jordan, C.H. & Zanna, M. (1999). How to read a journal article in social psychology. In R.F. Baumeister (Ed.), *The Self in Social Psychology* (pp. 461–70). Philadelphia, PA: Psychology Press.

Kant, I. ([1784] 1991). *Perpetual Peace: A Philosophical Sketch*. In H. Reiss (Ed.), *Political Writings* (pp. 93–130). Cambridge: Cambridge University Press.

Kim, E.H., Hogge, I., Ji, P., Shim, Y.R., & Lothspeich, C. (2014). Hwa-Byung among middle-aged Korean women: Family relationships, gender-role attitudes, and self-esteem. *Health Care for Women International* 35, 495–511.

Kim, J.S. (2001). Daughters-in-law in Korean caregiving families. *Journal of Advanced Nursing*, 36(3), 399–408.

Landrum, R.E. (2008). *Undergraduate Writing in Psychology: Learning to Tell the Scientific Story*. Washington, DC: APA.

Lipson, C. (2005). *How to Write a BA Thesis: A Practical Guide from Your First Ideas to Your Finished Paper*. Chicago, IL: University of Chicago Press.

Locke, L., Silverman, S., & Spirduso, W. (2010). *Reading and Understanding Research* (3rd ed.). Thousand Oaks, CA: Sage.

Lyng, S. (1990). Edgework: A social psychological analysis of voluntary risk taking. *American Journal of Sociology* 95(4), 851–86.

Machi, L.A. & McEvoy, B.T. (2012). *The Literature Review: Six Steps to Success*. Thousand Oaks, CA: Corwin.

Mill, J.S. (1997). On liberty. In A. Ryan (Ed.), *Mill* (pp. 41–132). New York: W.W. Norton.

Miller, A.B. (2009). *Finish Your Dissertation Once and for All!: How to Overcome Psychological Barriers, Get Results, and Move on With Your Life*. Washington, DC: APA.

Moffitt, T. (1993a). Adolescence-limited and life-course-persistent antisocial behavior: A developmental taxonomy. *Psychological Review* 100(4), 674–701.

Moffitt, T. (1993b). The neuropsychology of conduct disorder. *Development and Psychopathology* 5, 135–151.

Muir, W.K. (1977). *Police: Street Corner Politicians*. Chicago, IL: University of Chicago Press.

Noland, R.L. (1970). *Research and Report Writing in the Behavioral Sciences*. Springfield, IL: Charles C. Thomas.

Oliver, M.B. & Armstrong, G.B. (1995). Predictors of viewing and enjoyment of reality-based and fictional crime shows. *Journalism & Mass Communication Quarterly* 72(3), 559–70.

Osmond, A. (2013). *Academic Writing and Grammar for Students*. London: Sage.

Owen, J.J. (1999). Church and state in Stanley Fish's antiliberalism. *American Political Science Review* 93(4), 911–24.

Piquero, A.R., Farrington, D.P., Nagin, D.S., & Moffitt, T.E. (2010). Trajectories of offending and their relation to life failure in late middle age: Findings from the Cambridge Study in Delinquent Development. *Journal of Research in Crime and Delinquency* 47(2), 151–73.

Postman, N. (1985). *Amusing Ourselves to Death: Public Discourse in the Age of Show Business*. New York: Penguin Books.

Pritchard, D. & Hughes, K.D. (1997). Patterns of deviance in crime news. *Journal of Communication* 47(3), 49–67.

Rawls, J. (1971). *A Theory of Justice*. Cambridge, MA: Harvard University Press.

Rayner, K. & Pollatsek, A. (1989). *The Psychology of Reading*. Hillsdale, NJ: Lawrence Erlbaum Associates.

Ridley, D. (2012). *The Literature Review: A Step-by-Step Guide for Students*. London: Sage.

Rudestam, K.E. (2007). *Surviving Your Dissertation: A Comprehensive Guide to Content and Process* (3rd ed.). Thousand Oaks, CA: Sage.

Rudestam, K.E. & Newton, R.R. (2001). *Surviving Your Dissertation: A Comprehensive Guide to Content and Process*. Thousand Oaks, CA: Sage.

Salfati, C.G. (2000). The nature of expressiveness and instrumentality in homicide: Implications for offender profiling. *Homicide Studies* 4(3), 265–93.

Sampson, R.J. (1987). Urban black violence: The effect of male joblessness and family disruption. *American Journal of Sociology* 93, 348–82.

Shumaker, D.M. & Prinz, R. (2000). Children who murder: A review. *Clinical Child and Family Psychology Review* 3(2), 97–115.

Silvia, P. (2007). *How to Write a Lot*. Washington, DC: APA.

Strauss, A. 1987. *Qualitative Analysis for Social Scientists*. Cambridge: Cambridge University Press.

Strunk, W. Jr & White, E.B. (1979). *The Elements of Style* (3rd ed.). Needham Heights, MA: Allyn & Bacon.

Thapa, A., Cohen., J., Guffey, S., & Higgins-D'Alessandro, A. (2013). A review of school climate research. *Review of Educational Research* 83(3), 357–85.

Usoof-Thowfeek, R., Janoff-Bulman, R., & Tavernini, J. (2011). Moral judgments and the role of social harm: Differences in automatic versus controlled processing. *Journal of Experimental Social Psychology* 47, 1–6.

Vipond, D. (1996). *Success in Psychology: Writing and Research for Canadian Students*. Toronto: Harcourt Brace & Company.

Wallace, M. & Wray, A. (2011). *Critical Reading and Writing for Postgraduates*. London: Sage.

White, H.R., Bates, M.E., & Buyske, S. (2001). Adolescence-limited versus persistent delinquency: Extending Moffitt's hypothesis into adulthood. *Journal of Abnormal Psychology* 110, 4, 600–9.

Wyller, T. (2005). The place of pain in life. *Philosophy* 80(3), 385–93.

Index